THE WALK
Footsteps of My Journey

by
Wayne Mabry

DORRANCE
PUBLISHING CO
EST. 1920
PITTSBURGH, PENNSYLVANIA 15238

Dorrance Publishing Co
585 Alpha Drive
Pittsburgh, PA 15238

Visit our website at www.dorrancebookstore.com

ISBN: 978-1-6491-3380-9
eISBN: 978-1-6491-3608-4

A s I begin to share some moments of my journey, I'll hopefully touch someone's life on both a positive and spiritual level. My journey set sail on November 19th in the year 1956 in a small all-black town named Mound Bayou, Ms. Born, the eldest child of Lee and Minnie Mabry. Weighing in at 8 lbs. 2 oz, I was held in high regards from my mom who was the only girl along with five brothers in her family. My father Lee who was a seventeen year paratrooper in the military was often relocated to different bases so we moved around a bit until he and my mom had our first home built in Mound Bayou in the 1960s. Though it wasn't a large home, it was full of memories from my early childhood years. One in particular was the fact that our house sat on top of huge concrete blocks and us living in tornado territory, I was terrified of the house being swept away during these heavy thunderstorms. Having a storm cellar was looked at as a luxury because very few homeowners had them or could afford one. Our first house was built by a local contractor, but my mom and dad finished most of the interior themselves along with a couple of friends. Our gas was kept in a large propane tank that was filled on a monthly schedule by a gas truck that provided that service. We lived in my grandmother's house on the next lot behind our new home was being built. There were accordion type doors instead of hinged swinging doors to make the best use of space, but me as a kid thought they were cool. Back in that era, most houses still had the old outhouse restrooms, so to have a complete bathroom was almost luxurious. In the area of town that we lived there was no underground sewage systems so you had to install a septic tank for the waste. I remember taking baths at my grandma's house in a standard number 10 metal tub where we had to heat your water on top of the stove to get enough water to bath in. By today's standards our little Jim Walter home would be compared to a small two-bedroom apartment. I remember my grandmother

Nellie Hopkins-Lloyd

Nellie Hopkins-Lloyd who along with my grandfather Benjamin Lloyd Sr. owned thirteen acres that they farmed on the outskirts of Mound Bayou, Mississippi.

Hometown

There they raised my mom and her brothers before having their house built on the north end of town. My memories of her were always working hard and ready to lend a hand helping others. She had this yellow & white '57 Chevrolet Bel-Air that I loved to ride in whenever she took me with her around town, remembering how large it seemed as a kid. She worked as a housekeeper for a prominent family in Cleveland, Mississippi and when she drove there to pick up her paycheck would always tell me to stay inside her car even though the children, she took care of would stand at their front door waving for me to get out. It was many years later before I understood why she always went to the rear of the house and not use the front entrance. Good times and a great woman, I miss you Grandma. Mom told me that I used to make my brother Lee who was about four years younger, play with me by running and knocking him over, waiting for him to sit up again then running over him knocking him down again. I was an aggressive child and had to learn to channel that free spirit. In reading my story I hope to share some of my core beliefs and wisdom that I've gathered along this journey that I have been on since my birth, also hope that my story will inspire someone who's walking out their own journey as my way of planting a few positive seeds along my path and paying respect to some of the guardian angels sent to share a few brief moments with me showing me the right stepping stones to take as I continue on my walk. While continuing my walk I have grown to understand what having dreams, believing in those dreams, believing in yourself and having faith enough to take the steps necessary to achieve the goals and dreams you've set in front of you means to me. My message in this story is to strengthen your faith, believe in yourself and move forward and be that change you want to see in the world. Stay blessed!

Dedicated to My Mom

Chapter 1

There were always a group of neighborhood girls who stopped by our house so my mom could fix their hairdos. I thought she was more of a beautician rather than the phlebotomist and nurses aid work she performed at the community hospital. It was a special treat for me because while the girls waited for their turn in the chair, they played records on our little turntable and danced to the music from Motown. Usually turning into a dance contest which was very entertainment for a young boy in elementary school, that's probably where I first got the idea of owning my own night club. I can still picture them wearing the miniskirts, hip huggers, bobby sox and penny loafers looking like models on the runway. I would imagine them having cocktails and just letting their hair down, but that thought was always interrupted by the smell of burning hair coming from the kitchen as Mom heated up the straightening comb and curling irons that she used. During those days my brother and I really learned to enjoy dancing because the girls would pull us out on the living room floor to dance with them. They taught us a lot and soon after I began using music as a form of therapy as I found out it could be soothing or exhilarating depending on the style and tempo. While my mom fixed hair, we had our next door neighbor we called Ms. Bannie who was an excellent cook and you would think she ran a restaurant because every Sunday after church there would be cars lined up along the highway waiting their turn to get in her driveway to pick up the fried chicken dinners that she sold for $5.00 each. We hated it because the traffic would interrupt our evening football games in the front yard, being that her driveway was the southern end zone and our driveway was the northern end zone. It would be hell to pay if you hit anyone's vehicle with the ball. Even though we weren't happy with the Sunday traffic interrupting our games, I was inspired to become an entrepreneur myself so I began drawing designs on my schoolmate's clothing during high school and

My Elementary School

making money. She also sold sweet potato, egg and pecan pies all year long. It was impressive how much money she would make on the weekend, all cash and tax free. We often had to deal with rodents that would find their way into our house looking for food and a place to possibly build a nest, so I was put in charge of baiting and setting mouse traps in different areas of the house in an attempt to capture them and this huge field rat who had made a hole just large enough to get into the kitchen under the sink. At first we didn't realize how big this rat was because it would clean the food off the traps almost like a game until I got a much bigger trap like the ones used to capture animals much larger and put peanut butter on it for bait and anchored it to the floor of the kitchen cabinet. After eventually catching the rat by its hind leg my mom told me to burn it alive so the smell of its burning fur would act as a deterrent for the other rodents that were coming in the house. This rat was approximately eighteen inches nose to end of tail, so it was my biggest catch as a young kid. You probably would think that I was afraid of the task I'd been given, but even at a young age stood in our kitchen holding up this fresh catch and burning the fur just like Mom had instructed. That method must have worked because after fixing the hole the huge rat used to get into never had a problem with rodents after that. A few years after my mouse mystery was solved, I had an encounter with a huge wolf spider that had crawled into my pants leg overnight somehow, and upon running my hand in the leg of my pants to flip it inside out was bitten on my thumb. I just remember the excruciating pain and how it scared me when it crawled out of my pant leg and onto my bed. Picking up one of my shoes I hit it but only stunned it long enough to take one of my mom's hat pins and running it through its torso and placing the dazed spider on top of a huge fire ant bed to let them have a go at it. My thumb throbbed most of that day and sat in my classes wondering what was happening to my buddy the spider and if I would suffer any ill effects from the bite. First thing I did after making it home from school was to run to our backyard to see what these giant fire ants had done and to my delight they had taken all of its legs off. The hair pin that I used was long enough to keep the spider anchored to the ant bed as they dismantled its legs. I understand that everything has a place on the food chain, but when you cross paths with me, I intend to be the survivor. Looking back, I think that was a 'Foodie' at heart because there weren't many dishes that I wouldn't completely devour going back to the big tubes of bologna and cheese and other food items

My Dad

we received as a subsidy from the government once a month. Anytime my mom would leave the house I would raid the kitchen making double and triple decker sandwiches with thick slices of the bologna and cheese and when there was no meat, a triple decker syrup sandwich would do with a big mason jar of sugar water to wash it all down. My reasoning was that the more food I consumed the more weight I could gain to play football in high school. One day she left going to town and I made a bee line to the kitchen to construct one of my masterpiece sandwiches out of bologna, cheese, and about eight little gherkin pickles. Before completely devouring the sandwich, I hear Mom return and all I could think about was getting rid of the evidence, so I chugged down the rest of this sandwich not completely chewing everything up. I escaped getting caught at that time and went back outside to play, but later that evening my mom and dad took us to the drive-in theater in Cleveland and about halfway through the movie I started feeling sick to my stomach but didn't say a word. My brother saw how much pain I was in and told my mom and when she asked me what was wrong it was like my body confessed as I vomited all over the back seat and floor of the car. At this point not able to sit up, I could hear her saying that she could see why I was sick from the chunks of bologna and pickles

3

most with just the end bit off were spayed everywhere. They ended up rushing me back to the hospital in Mound Bayou where I was admitted and kept overnight which didn't help matters at all plus me fighting with the nurses who tried to administer an IV tube and take blood samples until Mom entered the room and threatened to knock me out if I didn't pipe down. I loved going through the hospital watching the doctors and nurses performing their crafts but being on the receiving end of the treatment changed the way I looked at hospitals after that. Before I enjoyed going into our family doctor's office and looking at all of his books on the human anatomy which lasted until my high school years taking biology. The best part of biology was dissecting the animal cadavers we used for class and getting a high percentage of our grades from our displays.

 My community was like a village, everyone looking out for each other whenever there was a neighbor in need and along with that of course came the never-ending eyes watching any mischief I might have decide to entertain myself with. I vividly remember not liking this added feature at all, learning at a very young age of timing out any bad behavior as to not be seen by those ever-present eyes. School days for me were happy times in the early years. Mostly enjoyable was lunch, recess and physical activities. I've always loved my Super Heroes and began drawing what I someday wanted to become as I grew up. Always impressed by how strong & powerful they were, but at the same time they used their powers for good deeds. During my days at school my teachers would constantly catch me drawing my Super Heroes during class and thinking that I wasn't paying attention to what was going on would call my name and ask me to tell the class what had just been covered. Rising to the occasion I'd answer their questions and go right back to drawing up my paper for school which was bought in reams because of how much I went through drawing. Upon seeing my persistence of drawing one of my third grade teachers told my mom that she should think about getting me in some type of Art school, which there weren't any near where we lived so as the years went by I became better at what was an early passion for me, an es-

cape from the ordinary if you will because of my ability to sketch anything in my head. Soon I began to participate in drawing contest at school and from that started to help with designing the school's bulletin boards, which was even more fun because you got excused from class and was kept up to date on any lessons missed. As the following years went by and my drawing skills improved, opportunities opened up where I began to actually get paid for my artwork. These opportunities continued through high school and even after I left college at Jackson State University. Growing up in the south most of us had a passion for football, it was like religion as it gave us another way to express ourselves, release some aggressions, challenge ourselves in the face of adversity and learn the importance of teamwork when it comes to tackling life's situations that we would face as life's journey continued. I particularly loved the physical and aggressive nature of the game where you engaged in man to man battles of eleven men until the best team was victorious reminding me of the gladiators of the past without the weapons of course. I had watched this game on television since a youngster. I began to envision myself someday playing this sport well after collage, so I guess you could call it an obsession with the game. And with that I began to train every morning before I left for school, doing pushups, sit-ups and jumping jacks. During this period in the seventies there weren't a lot of fitness gurus that I was able to meet, let along watch on television. But I soaked up every muscle mag, watched the few fitness shows on TV in those days and dreamed of developing a powerful physique as close to my Super Heroes as humanly possible. Being the eldest of five kids, a lot of responsibility was asked of me by my mom as she struggled to provide most of our needs while working long hours at our community hospital. We always had a chore list to complete that she would stick on the refrigerator and if things weren't done when Mom got home from work, well let's just say there would be hell to pay. I remember around the age of twelve she started teaching me how to cook, sew, iron, do laundry and generally run the house. Now at that young age learning these chores was the last thing on my mind and though I did my best rebellious behavior Mom won those battles hands down, and in the process taught me skills that I'm still using today. For that I say "Thank You!" Even though her nickname was the Warden, she was only attempting to raise us to be respectful, honest and responsible kids. She never knew about her nickname until many years later. We also had a vegetable garden back in Mississippi that was always in need of TLC to stay on top of maintenance and harvesting, so we spent a lot of evenings helping Mom tend to this place we called the "Truck patch". She was constantly explaining why going through this whole process would help provide an abundance of fresh fruits and vegetables for the family during those cold winters that showed up like clockwork every December. I'm talking about winters so cold

My High School Days

that our water lines would often burst leaving us without running water, so we would store water in containers just in case during those frigid days, gas barely burning on our appliances, power lines knocked down from ice accumulating on the trees causing limbs to break and the ground being as hard as asphalt or the snow drifts so high around our house that we had to climb out a window to get outside. But through it all we didn't miss any meals, I guess all those days planting seeds, cultivating, harvesting and preparing those crops was just part of the process she wanted to instill in us when we were kids. I used to ask Mom why every time she was cooking during those cold winter days my friends would show up at the door and she would invite them in and offer them a plate or a bowl of whatever we were eating and I would be looking at them like, you guys never offered to help when we were working in the truck patch, as a matter of fact they thought it was funny because we would be chopping and pulling weeds wearing straw hats and gloves in the summer heat, or come harvest time had our baskets to pick the crops to be shelled, prepared and put in our chest freezer for food during the winter, but would be more than happy to sit and eat. After everyone else had gone outside she would say to me, baby it's the Christian thing to do being hospitable even though you may be looking at it as me giving away the food we were supposed to eat. She would say we would be blessed for the acts of kindness and hospitality. Till this day it reminds me of that whole village raising a child mindset that most people had back then. Even when it came down to disciplining children, any adult could whip your butt if you got out of line and then upon telling the parents usually ended with another worst whipping. It was like our modern-day neighborhood watch, but with the focus on the kids. There were a few other rules around our house that sounded like "old folks" talk to me because every elderly person you'd run across had the same lines of advice, for example washing your face and brushing your teeth before you step to the table for breakfast or if you had to be told to shut up more than once usually a backhand or whatever could be thrown your way followed, being at home before sun down, if you messed it up clean it up, spraying the house for mosquitoes every night so we could get a good night's sleep, you'll reap what you sow and so forth and so on. I remember calling our bedroom cell block D, with my brother Lee as my cellmate. To me, we were serving a sentence of hard labor with no chance of parole. But the truth was that though we were poor, we didn't suffer for lack of housing, clothing, food and love. But I always looked at it as "tough love", because there was no pampering like we see today when it comes to raising kids. Mom had a saying passed down from her mother that every tub has to sit on its own bottom. Now she never explained out right what it meant but when I became an adult it became very clear what the saying meant. "You are responsible for you" is the message I've gotten from Mom's cliché and try to pass it on as I travel along this journey. When it came down to discipline nothing was held back when we got out of line, and believe me when I say it happened on a regular basis. And to make matters worse, we had to braid at least three branches from the neighbor's willow tree for her to dish out our punishment. The catch 22 to that situation was that if the switch broke and she had to go and braid the switches the punishment lasted that much longer. When she didn't use a switch, an extension cord would do just as well which I hated because of the definitive marks it left on your body so everyone knew that you had gotten whipped with an extension cord. During these punishments my brother Lee would practice improving his fortieth time, as

My Elementary School

he would run outside every chance he got and our neighbors got a little entertainment from her chasing him around the house and the neighborhood as you could hear them cheering her on. Hopefully you can see why I gave her the nickname "Warden". Even back then when we had our play time, it too was a little bit different. Most of my time was spent modeling toys out of the clay like mud that came from the soil in that area because we didn't have a lot of toys growing up. But I could vision something I wanted to play with, usually army tanks, dump trucks, swords, and of course my comic heroes. Funny thing is after all of the time and effort I put into building my toys out of mud, they usually got destroyed quickly as I played kind of rough with them so things just didn't hold up as well as expected. Even the rooftop of our house was part of an obstacle course as we would have flying contest jumping off to the ground holding a sheet like paratroopers and sort of grading ourselves on the landings, not even considering the possibility of breaking a bone or worst in doing so. There were days where we would have races rolling old tires filled with dirt to see who could not only win but make the biggest dust clouds and having someone ride inside the tire, or having jousting wars on our bicycles with broom sticks until I destroyed the rim and damaged one of my neighbor's with a direct hit to his sternum, after which no one else wanted to joust saying that I was too intense and competitive. Our neighbors William and Zelus were the first kids in the area who had the Hot Wheels race set and Lee and I spent hours at their house playing with them until one of us got a yell from Mom to do chores. Most hot summer days would find us down on the banks of the river that flowed behind our house where we would strip down to our underwear jumping into it fighting off the leeches and snakes that were always around, and it's where I learned to swim because the community pool was kept empty during the brutally hot and humid summers because you had to belong to a certain club, but the story spread around town was that there wasn't a certified lifeguard which we never believed. Also, the river was a place of refuge from the eyes of the village except one elderly man whose property ran to the edge of the river. He didn't like the sound of us having fun and would sometimes threaten us with his shotgun. This scenario continued for years until one particular time he started firing his shotgun causing one of my cousins to severely injure his privates on a barbed wire

High School

fence as we ran to get out of his line of sight. And after having to explain what happened along the river bank we were told not to play down there again. Those words fell upon deft ears because we had cousins who lived just across the river and the quickest way to their house was to cross the river. When we could get enough guys together a sandlot football game usually followed, the trick was to end up on the more dominate team, one who hated losing like I did. Sometimes it worked perfectly and other times it didn't, but those instances were when you seemed to have just an extra edge to your game to make up for any shortcomings in talent or competitive spirit. I had my own mental list of guys who I wanted to go battle with from the neighborhood like Adrian, Berlin, Edwin, Lee, Rommel, Ray and Ernest who I always hoped would end up on my team. My brother always wanted to be on my team because he knew the punishment he would take being on opposite sides, so avoided me at all cost calling me a Mad Man. It just depended who the captains were picking the players, but after the pomp and circumstance we got down to some bloody, hard knocks football. My ritual back then was to wrap each of my forearms with the bath towels that I took from the linen closet, hoping Mom would never find out because I would have gotten beaten up more than in the game. A good tape job followed on the towels leaving my arms looking like I had a cast on them and once finished and tested I was ready to go to war with whoever lined up in front of me. There were no referees so the games relied on honesty and fortitude and would go on until either one team quit or a few of us got called home to do chores or to make a run down to the community store. Back at home there were also the occasional fights with my brother when he didn't want to complete his chores on Mom's list, knowing that we would both be punished so the furniture usually got rearranged and not in a nice way. One memorable fight was based around the chore list and his refusal to complete his part and during our battle he grabbed a pencil stabbing me in my shoulder and breaking off the lead which just intensified the fight to the point that my sister Jacqueline got scared and ran next door and got Ms. Bannie one of our neighbors to come over and break us up. Surprisingly I never had any ill effects from the pencil lead in my shoulder, but my sister got the worst of it when I hung her out of a bedroom window by her ankles for bringing the neighbor into the picture because it was bad enough when we were playing outside and they always had something to say to us and bringing the neighbor inside our house to me was the deal breaker. And yes, I was severely punished for my actions but to me it was worth it as I sent a message to her to stay out of my business and stay out of my way. I called the bedroom that my brother and I shared Cell Block D, which was looked at as a place of sanctuary inside our house. Like with any block there were some rules to follow such as 'No Chatter' because I always had my little stereo playing one of several 8 tracks I had to put my mind in a meditative state. Every time Lee came to the room, he wanted to flop on the foot of my bed chattering and giggling interrupting my Zen moment, so I implemented the 'No Chatter' rule. Another rule implemented was the 'Stay on Your Side' which was because of him sitting on my bed instead of his, the closet was also split down the middle with each of us having our separate clothes hamper. There were designated wash days and if your dirty clothes weren't put in the laundry room to be washed, you had to do without until the next wash day. We shared a chest of drawers for our clothes and my drawers were always organized, where Lee could care less about being organized so when he ran out of clothes he waited until I wasn't around and helped himself to my clothes. This prompted me to implement the 'Stay out My Drawers' rule, which was constantly breeched and the cause of a few brawls up in cell block D. Another incident where the furniture got rearranged was when my dad's brother Robert stopped by the house one Saturday and he had a way of irritating me to no end because he would always put his hand on top of my head when saying hello and I would say to him that I wasn't a puppy. I would tell him constantly not to play with my head but it seemed to amuse him the more I said it. So this particular day he caught me in a bad mood and being a big wrestling fan put a move on him flipping him to the floor but in the process his feet hit our patio door completely shattering it and I went back into my room. I thought my dad was going to kill him as he cussed up a storm never saying a word to me because he had heard me warning my uncle Robert not to mess with me. After he helped my dad tape heavy plastic over the broken patio door until the glass could be replaced never touched my head again and apologized for sending me into a rage, causing us to move some furniture around. Through our many disagreements at home, when we went out in public were a united front watching the others back because in our minds it was us against the world because we lived on the northern edge of town which was called the North End and being just outside of the city limits were looked at like outcast. I took it as a challenge so when we played sports it was the guys from the North End against the guys from other areas around town. Respect was earned over the years as guys would leave battered and bruised after our competitions because of the rough edge that we played with and the chip we had on our shoulders. One of our general rules was no crying on the field or urt or you got replaced and probably wouldn't be allowed to participate anymore. Plus, there was no running to tattle to any adults when things got rough because we handled the issues ourselves. There was a large field back between our house and the river with very tall grass where we make forts to hide out in, sometimes playing adult games when the opportunity presented itself. The trick was not to walk directly to the fort but go out of the way, not to give away the exact location because like I said before someone was always peeping out their windows trying to keep an eye on what we were doing, I just called it being nosey. Our front yard was covered in clover which the honey bees loved to feed on and we had always been told never to play outside without some shoes on, but on the occasions when those words fell upon deft ears we often suffered from bee stings to our feet and hands or stepped on nails and broken glass. Now I thought having swollen feet would prevent me from having to attend church on Sundays but Mom would just say, stuff your feet in those wing tips some kind of way because you're not missing church. Imagine the embarrassment of limping around at church with sore feet, even sitting around in those stiff shoes made them swell even more until it went away several days later. And staying home from school was not an option, as a matter of fact we only got to stay home if we had the flu so other than that you got your breakfast, gathered your books and either caught the bus that ran in our neighborhood or walked the half mile to school from our house just up the road on US Highway 61 which ran all the way to Memphis, Tennessee. I would take the walk even with my swollen feet because I could squeeze in the morning workout before going to homeroom for the morning roll call. Remember when I described the eyes of the village watching us, well imagine trying to sneak out of church to make a candy run which was to a store across the railroad tracks in front of our church, sneak back into church and try to enjoy the candy without anyone hearing you tearing the wrapping off. The ushers would be the ones who busted us because they watch over the youth like hawks and would walk up, tap you on the shoulder and ask for whatever treat you had. This was some of the most fun and stressful times because there would be hell to pay if you got caught and sheer joy when you were successful in eating your candy undiscovered. Again, the watching eyes of the village. The most opportune time for the candy run was between Sunday school classes and the start of morning worship services, so would see us leaving in different directions from church trying not to give away our intentions of making a bee line to the nearby store. It was funny how the owners of the store greeted us because they knew from the way we were dressed that we were supposed to be in church, but happily took our monies and wished us well. We attended a Baptist church and were often time there from around 9:30 a.m. until 2:00 p.m. which seemed like an eternity to me because by the time we returned home changed out of our church clothes, ate dinner most of the day was gone leaving very little playtime before coming inside to prepare for school the next day. I remember dreaming about breaking that cycle and just having the freedom to pursue my own interest and how ritualistic everything seemed, but as I got older realized that most of our lives are filled with some type of ritual and as bad as I hate to admit it helps keep order in my life today.

Chapter 2

Life was definitely an adventure around the Mabry compound and juggling school work, chores and playtime was a full plate. School for me was just a social gathering where you got a chance to hang out with friends you wouldn't ordinarily see on a daily basis, forming bonds that still last to this day and time. Most of the curriculum studies we had didn't really prepare us for real life situations, but the teachers followed what they were given to teach. I used to ask some of my teachers why we were given these school curriculums that weren't focused on people like us which I never got a satisfactory answer to. But being a dreamer, I have always kept myself entertained, sometimes earning me the duties of cleaning all the erasers from the chalk boards after school where you had to beat these erasers against a large tree on the edge of campus until they were clean. Coming home covered in chalk was a message to the parents that you had gotten into trouble during the day at school. So after a few times with the erasers I decided that changing my behavior in class had to be adjusted and found other means of amusing myself without having the eraser side effects, especially the chalk in my hair which meant having to wash it every time when usually I washed my hair once a week. Recess back then was like the call of the wild, as it became survival of the fittest and the merry-go-round was the proving ground. Always looking for a way to physically exert myself tried to be one of the ones turning the huge merry-go-round out across campus and coaxing as many girls to join us as would fit on the ride. Thrilling them with how fast we could get the ride turning and making them scream with fear of falling off if they didn't maintain a tight grip into the surrounding dirt. During my junior high school days, most of my time excused from class was helping to create backdrops for the school plays where I really started to appreciate my drawing skills as I was asked to draw nature scenes with the wildlife included, which was a challenge readily accepted. I also spent many days with my good friend Cornelius preparing popcorn for the sporting events at the high school which we enjoyed because we ate plenty of it during the preparation which we looked at as the perks for our time and effort. Also during these years, I became interested in playing the trumpet because of a famous jazz trumpeter named Miles Davis so I auditioned for the Jr. High band and remembering how I fell in love with the instrument with its' screaming brassy sound. By the time I graduated from high school, I had become the lead trumpeter in our stage band. As I approached my high school years, things seemed to intensify as school activities, the chore lists and other responsibilities grew. There were no excuses for bringing home anything less than a B on our report cards. Falling short of that carried a heavy penalty, including "Lockdown" where all you could do was go to school, complete your chores eat dinner and go in your room and study. Don't think for a second that she waivered with the punishment, it usually would last a few weeks or until the next report card period so trying to accomplish good grades was instilled in us at a young age. In 1969 when the gulf coast was hit by hurricane Camille, we suffered tremendous flooding in the flat delta where we lived. All of the rivers crested from the tremendous amount of rain that fell during the thunderstorms and tornadoes that followed her through the entire state of Mississippi. People were driving up to our houses in boats checking to see if everyone was okay, I just remember the water being so high that it came up to the threshold of our doors. Had the rain lasted much longer I believe our house even sitting up on those huge concrete blocks would have flooded. There were some houses that did suffer flood damage but thankfully there weren't any casualties in the town, even though down on the gulf shores there were a total of 259 deaths from this category 5 hurricane. It was at that time the second highest rated hurricane in US history. Going from junior high to high school in 1971 was an exciting jump for me as opportunities increased to spread my wings a little bit more. My pursuit of art, music and sports broaden my visions of escaping what I called Alcatraz. It took me until my sophomore year to make the football team often told that I was too short to play linebacker or even pursue it after high school. Coach Bradfield was the only one who kept encouraging me to stick with the position I wanted to play regardless of what my head coach told me. Looking back, I regret taking the advice of those coaches who didn't have my best interest in mind. Keeping busy was a way to escape the reality of how poor we were and how bad economically the area was and just kept me dreaming of living somewhere else. We used to say as kids that we were 'PO' poor because we couldn't afford the 'OR'. Our stepdad Richard use to take us out to his parent's house out in the country east of town to visit his parents who owned a farm. He and I never got along because since my dad had left, I considered myself the man of the house, but his parents were nice and I respected them. It's on their farm that I discovered a whole different world than what I was used to, rising before sunrise to feed the animals, checking the chicken's nest for fresh eggs, driving the tractor to plow the fields, watching them breed the livestock and target shooting with a rifle at the lake. Though intriguing as this life was, I knew right away it wasn't for me, but each visit was an escape from the chore list at home and we could eat as much food as we could, which was my favorite memory of the trips to the farm. My mom had two kids with him, my sister Regina and brother Fernardus. I remember us receiving government surplus food, which was given out once a month so it was rationed strictly by our Mom so we would hopefully make it last until the next supplies would come. From an educational standpoint I maintained around a B grade average throughout my high school years, but to me school was more of a social gathering for most of us because if we weren't in attendance usually that meant you were working in the fields helping the family to make ends meet which quite a few of my schoolmates had to do from time to time. Agriculture, factories and retail were the main avenues of employment around my town and I had no desire to do any of those. My artistic skills were a means of making a little pocket money along with mowing yards which was a regular part of our chore list, especially during spring and summer months. The lawnmower we mowed the yards with was an annual Christmas gift from our dad instead of toys. Mostly our gifts consisted of clothing to finish out the school year, fruit baskets and coloring books so we figured out real early that Santa Claus was just folklore not a real person at all. As a matter of fact, we would always catch Mom trying to sneak in the occasional toys that she got for us which was not much especially with the wages she made being less than twenty thousand dollars per year for her entire career in the medical industry. Even though we didn't have much around Christmas or any other holiday Mom always enjoyed decorating our house. One particular Christmas season she chose a smaller tree that sat on top of this big television in the living room. In my determination to grab some of the sweet treats that were assembled around the base of the tree, I pulled myself to the top of the television holding on to the back edge. My hanging on must have started it to fall forward and the next thing I remember was screaming as the heavy metal television, the tree and all the decorations fell on top of me. After checking me out for any damages Mom told me my situation was caused by my decision to get into something that I knew I wasn't supposed to, she didn't even whip my butt and I'm guessing that me escaping injury should've been lesson enough for me on that day. My dad who worked for a general contractor after he got out of the military would often let me drive the cement mixer truck. As a matter of fact, that was where my love for big diesel vehicles was born. He would explain to me the importance of hand and eye coordination to keep it in between the lines, even though to me this truck was a monster he would say to me just steer it like you would a pickup truck. I enjoyed the driving lessons but had no intentions of doing this for a living. My summation of things looking back was that we were being taught in a lot of ways to be independent, to be strong willed and respectable individuals which I'm very thankful for now. As I look at today's society, much of the tough love and community outreach isn't as prevalent as back then, you know the common cliché (times have changed). I think it's the people who've changed their morals to flow with what "society" dictates as to what's acceptable or trending and you can see the results in today's society where values like respect and honesty are a rarity. Those values I learned about pursuing your dreams, working hard, being accountable, honest and fair still carry me forward today and I try to share them at every opportunity. My four years of high school seemed like an eternity because this is when I got my urge to move to California after watching both the Raiders and the Rose Bowl games on television admiring the weather, the terrain with those beautiful beaches, majestic mountains, the tropical vegetation and people wearing shorts and tank tops in winter. Shortly after I kept trying to persuade my mom to move us there where she could get a job in the medical industry making a lot more money, and her reply to me was "baby this is home" made me decide right then that as soon as I graduated it was California here I come. Anyway, I made the best of my opportunities throughout my high school days keeping myself busy doing just about anything to not be stuck at home doing chores. Aside from my artistic skills I played football, built furniture in woodshop, excelled in mechanical drawing and participated in the school bands. Being kind of a loner, I still had a few close friends who I constantly carried on some mischief with both at school and around town. I remember some of our teachers telling us that they knew we were up to something every time we were seen together, and we never disputed the accusations but didn't admit to anything either because we lived by a code of silence amidst our group. With each passing year my quest to get to California grew stronger and stronger to the point I was just going through the motions with most of my activities looking forward to graduation day. Prom season was always intriguing with the pomp and circumstances that come with it, building up to the climax of Prom night where you would get sharply dressed and take a date out on the town after the school's ceremonies before time to have her back home. Here goes my senior year and I was so excited for Prom season so I could begin the quest of taking some young lady as my date, picking her up in my mom's car and having the time of my life. If you remember the punishments I mentioned earlier in this story, by this time my mom knew the best way to punish me was keeping me from one of my many activities to really make her point. Well making a long story short after securing my date, washing and waxing the car, renting my tux and buying the corsage my mom tells me a few hours before I was supposed to pick up my date for the Prom that I should call her parents to let them know that I wouldn't be picking their daughter up after all. This was a timely way of punishing me for something I had gotten in trouble for earlier, so she waited until Prom night to spring this on me. Let me tell you, that phone call was the hardest thing to do up until that point in my life. My date's Father was a minister but you wouldn't have thought so by his conversation with me and then her mom finished me off. This young lady that I was supposed to take to the Prom hardly spoke to me the rest of the school year and even during our years in college at Jackson State. But the lesson had been taught to me by Mom that she could pull my card anytime she pleased. During my senior year because of my artistic and writing skills my fellow classmates thought it would be quite the joke to nominate me for class secretary. I tried everything to get out of because I hated politics and wanted nothing to do with student government. After all the voting was over and tallied up, I barely edged out the young lady who ran against me who I felt should've been class secretary, so I reluctantly took on my duties as secretary and made the best of what was supposed to have been a bad situation for me. We had several school dances in the gymnasium throughout the year and the best part to me was performing with the jazz band playing the top hits of that period, watching our schoolmates busting moves and really enjoying themselves. Hell, even a few of the teachers showed us some of their moves which was like a seal of approval to our funky tunes. Finally, graduation rolls around and I couldn't wait to take that last walk across the stage to receive my diploma and put that part of my journey behind me. On our senior class trip to Houston, Texas we had a great time seeing the sights of the city and mostly the parties at the hotel where we stayed. One night before we left during the finale party security came and told us to shut it down because some of the other guests were complaining about the noise. At the time we said it was because we didn't invite them and that incident put a damper on our party. The next morning, we boarded our charter buses heading back to Mound Bayou. To my knowledge our senior class had been the only one told by the principal that he was glad to see move on, guessing that his statement in front of our parents stemmed from the student protest we exercised in front of the school earlier that year that we called a 'Sit Out'. We had enough of the dress codes that they tried to enforce on us, so like the rebels most of us were came to school wearing everything banned by this code. I cut one leg off of my jeans up to the crotch and shredded the other leg from the bottom up to the crotch, cut a shirt where it looked like a halter top, wore one sandal and one regular shoe and sunglasses with a bandana tied around my afro. Everyone who had the courage to participate got suspended for three days, which meant three days of house parties because most of us had our classes taken care of and weren't worried about graduating. Graduation day was one of those warm and humid May afternoons and even with all the doors open in the gymnasium with the exhaust fans running still felt like a sauna, especially wearing our cap and gowns over our regular clothing. I would be doing my last performance with the concert band where the director gave me a trumpet solo in one of the songs we played as I pretended to be Miles Davis. To me it was an opportunity to give everyone there at the graduation ceremony something to remember me by on my way out of John F. Kennedy High School. It's funny how your plans can be turned upside down as in my case when after graduation I was sent to Milwaukee, Wisconsin to live with my uncle Benny and his family and to get a summer job before going to college the next fall at Jackson State University in Jackson, Mississippi. I didn't focus on going to college as much as I did landing a summer job to have my own money so I could pursue my dream of finally getting to that golden state on the West coast with its beautiful beaches and palm trees. I landed a job working at a restaurant where in a short period of time worked my way from grill master to cashier, which was my first official job ever. I was proud of my accomplishment when receiving that first check with my name on it. Most of my down time was spent hanging out with one of my cousins who graduated with me and went to visit a brother who also lived in Milwaukee. We would cruise around town in his brother's panel truck from the laundry service he owned which didn't bother us at all because we had wheels to go where ever we wanted. Hitting the freeway at times and driving from Milwaukee to Chicago and back was a typical joy ride for us just to take in the sites and grab a bite to eat. I never had a car during my time in school other than borrowing my parent's every now and then, so just being able to hit the road with my cousin was a treat giving me a new appreciation of not having to borrow my uncle's car especially to drive to Chicago. Even when going to visit Susan the girl I dated during that summer in Milwaukee walked way across town like I was taking a stroll to the grocery store, because it had become second nature to me from walking so much back home. The summer vacation went by too quickly as it was time for me to return to Mississippi for college and I remember being torn between respecting my mom's wishes of me getting a degree in Art or just going to pursue my dreams of getting to California. Long story short is I ended up attending Jackson State University from August of 1974 until the end of 1975 just a semester short of finishing my sophomore year. Looking back at that short period of time I got to travel to places I'd only seen on television while performing in the marching band and experience different cultures through the people on campus who came from cities all across the country. Upon my arrival for band camp in July which was much like football training camp, already had a good reputation because of the musicians from my high school who had already excelled in their music careers at Jackson State. The physical part of band camp didn't bother me as much as having to learn all of the music to be performed during the season and auditioning in front of the band directors in hopes of making the band. The reason we had to know our music by heart was because they didn't let you have music attached to the instruments when we performed, thus we could focus on the many dances and intricate formations we did on the football fields high stepping with our heels to the knees style. After the camp was complete, I was amazed to be awarded the eighth chair in the trumpet section of twenty-eight as a freshman, which the directors say was rarely done but I had good range and could project my sound while playing my trumpet. Thank you to my high school band director Mr. Strickland who always encouraged me to push myself to excel with my gift of music. At the same time, I had to mature quickly as I found out that even with your roommates and colleagues on campus lending support, you're still on your own when it came down to the decisions you made and the consequences that followed. After the partial scholarship I had in Art ran out following my first year it got kind of tough just to eat with not having money in my pockets, but one of my bandmates Eddie helped his dad out who was a brick mason on some jobs and asked if I wanted to make some quick cash. Working with my friend Eddie and his dad allowed me to keep money all the time, but that working experience stoked my desire to never be that broke again and make the move to California. Mom would send me boxes of canned goods and other food to campus to heat up on my hot plate in my dorm room because my food credit in the cafeteria ran out with my partial scholarship, so it was party time in my dorm room until everything had been consumed. I didn't mind it because those same dorm mates helped me through my rough times when they could. Our floor in the dorm was like my community back home. I felt a bit guilty because of the care packages my mom struggled to mail to me in school and knowing how little money she was making, so my attention on going to class began to fade and leaving college seemed like the

Competitive Body-building Days

next step for me, especially after what I went through with my art instructor who kicked me out of class for having a difference of opinion about techniques for drawing. My art instructor in grade school had shown me some techniques that worked with my style and honestly was light years ahead of my college professor, so we basically got into a situation over our philosophies. Those times really showed me to rely on my better judgements and truly stand on what I believed to be in the best interest for my life going forward. There were other students in our classroom that also had different opinions of his teaching methods, but somehow my style rubbed him the wrong way and I would stand up to him. I was inspired by some the people on campus that were living their dreams, names like Payton, Slater, Brazile and Young. Guys that I saw go on to play professional football after college, which further stoked the fire inside of me to set my sights on getting to California to do exactly the same thing in pursuing my dreams. One of my favorite uncles Andy used to always spend time with me and my brother Lee talking to us about the birds and the bees, which was great conversation to us being as young and impressionable as we were. We but loved hanging out with him to hear these stories and his personal experiences he had both survived and mostly enjoyed. Many times, confirming a lot of the teachings we got from Mom, but with a male's perspective also which we loved. I remember wearing some of his shoes that weren't quite my size while in high school because I hated the shoes Mom picked for us to wear and his style was more like what inspired me with my fashion choices going forward. We could also depend on him for a little pocket money, but we'd have to earn it by doing small chores at his house which never seemed to bother us because at home there were no monetary rewards just punishment for not doing them. He was a Navy veteran so his life was sort of methodical and scheduled like when he was in service, but he made it seem so natural. Using some of his methodology made my daily life more enjoyable also. Learning how to use my time more efficiently, keeping things organized and in their proper places. He had a newspaper route early in the mornings and I remember riding with him during the summers watching the hard work he put in just to deliver people's daily paper, but he'd always have a stogie in the corner of his mouth and always seemed so relaxed while running his paper route. One particular day he asks me if I wanted to try one, of course I said yes and he proceeded to cut and light one for me. Long story short, about halfway through my cigar I was so sick I couldn't sit up straight which he got quite a laugh out of. His exact words were, "I bet you won't smoke it like that again." In my enthusiasm to enjoy this cigar, I was inhaling it much like a cigarette and turned a shade of green I never want to see or experience again. He taught me afterward how to properly enjoy a cigar and till this day I give him a salute with every cigar I smoke. He also impressed me and my brother with how he held down two jobs and still found time to just relax, often sharing stories with us about him growing up with my mom and the four other brothers and the things they got in trouble for as kids. He taught my brother Lee and I how to pack our clothes in a suitcase like they did in the Navy by rolling everything like tubes so you could fit a lot into your suitcase, duffle bags or whatever you traveled with. Because our dad hadn't been around, he became my male role model. Andy often came to our rescue when we got in trouble but the most memorable one was the time my brother and I got kicked out of the house. Looking back on the events leading up to that infamous night around 11:30 when Mom took both our house keys, told us to pack our suitcases and get out of the house. I think we had pushed her to her limits as I had come back home from college and grew angrier every day thinking about my trek to California, so I gave her a hard time by not honoring the curfew she had set and really broke off any meaningful conversation, so she told us if you think life's so bad here at home just wait and see what's out in the streets. I remember asking her where we were supposed to go or sleep that night and her reply was, "I really don't care but you're getting the hell out of here and taking your brother with you since he seems to act like you." So we left the house walking toward town, but first we had to stash our suitcases somewhere out of sight until we figured out a plan. There was a church along the way and we figured what better place to hide our luggage for the night because no one hung out around churches, especially at those hours. After stashing our suitcases on the back porch of the nearby church we took to the railroad tracks that ran behind it to walk to town and find a spot to sleep for the night before hitchhiking to the city of Cleveland the next day which was where my uncle Andy had moved to ten miles away. Upon reaching town everything was closed except the bars and a cafe so we found a spot near a grocery store front on the main street with plenty of light to sleep for the night. We sat back to back so nothing or no one could sneak up on us, and other than a few stray dogs coming by we managed the hard cold concrete until morning when we took the train tracks to walk back to the church near our house to get the suitcases we'd stashed and began to hitchhike our way to our uncle's house in Cleveland. Once we reached his apartment and explained what went down at home, he and his wife agreed to let us stay there until he could persuade Mom to let us come back home. I think that time there with him and his wife must have seemed like an eternity because she hadn't been around us and I could sense her uneasiness. It took about a month as Mom was determined to stand her ground on her decision, meantime it was sort of like being on lockdown all over again because Cleveland was one of our rival cities in sports and just walking around town wasn't the smartest idea, so I remember just sitting on the stoop to his apartment for the entire time there and thinking about where I wanted my life to end up going forward. During this time my thoughts of leaving Mississippi and going to California took on a much stronger position in my mind, so I was very determined to make it there almost becoming obsessed with that vision. After my uncle somehow convinced Mom to allow us to return home, I had made up my mind that it was time for me to move on so I ended up staying with a schoolmate who just happened to be starting up a band with the hopes of going to California to compete for a spot on the Gong Show. But before all of these events could took place, my brother and I were picked up and moved to Memphis, Tennessee by our dad who Mom had called in an attempt to get us on the right track and hopefully bridge that gap created when he and my mom got divorced. He got a nice apartment in Barron Courts on the nicer side of town for us to live in while he worked on construction sites all across the state. As he tried to get to know us again he would take Lee and I shopping for clothes and shoes which put him in a state of shock when he got the bill for all the items we picked out because at this point we had no consideration of how expensive our clothes and shoes cost, especially if he was paying for them. And the store that I took him to was one of most famous clothing stores in Memphis for the type of fashion designs that we wanted to wear. My brother would always say that I was two brain cells short of retardation because he knew what my thinking was. So after my dad swallowed the bitter pill of taking us on a shopping spree and got my brother enrolled in school, tried to convince me to work with him on his construction projects. For the sake of earning my own money I went to one project remodeling a school where he was teaching me how to install hardwood floors in the gymnasium, but after wearing out the toes on a pair of shoes that I wore told him that I would find my own work and didn't return to the project the next week and asked him to cash me out. Being the drill sergeant type of guy that he was kept on me to aggressively look for work so I wouldn't start hanging around with the partyers that lived in our complex, because he knew a few of them were from my hometown so he already knew how that scenario was going to play out. He would say they were just wasting their lives away, but partying we did mostly at our friend's place. We kept the apartment where we stayed in immaculate condition and his favorite meal consisting of spaghetti, fish and cold beer when he returned home on Friday evenings. My brother and I would wait around until he finished eating knowing that he would be gone until Sunday evening, so we could do our weekend partying. Eventually I ran across this company who needed sales people to canvas neighborhoods selling publications for them and the only incentive for me accepting the job was the fact that their turnaround destination was California which had long been my destination. Upon hearing this I was ready to get started and couldn't wait to let my dad know I'd finally landed a job, but when I broke the news that I would be leaving heading for California he questioned my wanting to go across the country not knowing that this had been a dream of mine since back in high school. Finally, he came to grips with the idea because he saw my determination to be independent and carve my own path. I started work with my new employer and immediately got put with a team of sales people going door to door selling magazines and other publications. Talk about an experience I never expected nor will ever forget as we traveled from the state of Tennessee heading on a course to Los Angeles, there were days some of us didn't eat because we hadn't generated enough revenues from our sales. Plus, some of the female sales people were performing sex acts just to make their sales appear more lucrative which the owners of the company didn't seem to mind as long as your sales looked good at the end of the day. Here's where my journey took a wrong turn one day as we set out to make more sales, we were dropped off by a van in this quiet neighborhood in El Paso, Texas and as was customary got picked up late in the evenings at a predetermined location. After being dropped at our location for the day we would go out in different directions to canvas the neighborhood looking for potential sales. So I'm going from door to door on the street I had chosen trying to make my sales when I came across this particular house that had a Great Dane in their back yard standing as tall as the fence that scared the hell out of me because other than on television I'd never seen a dog of that size and especially up close and personal. I knock on the door of this house and a lady answers, I introduce myself and go right into my sales pitch when a man's voice sounded off from another room in the house telling the lady to have me get the hell off his property talking about selling magazines, but in my determination to get a sale from her didn't immediately walk away. The man's voice rang out again with more anger this time so she suggested that I should leave right now which I did seeing the fear in her eyes. As I began walking towards the next house there was a loud growl coming from behind me and as I turned to look here comes the dog from the house I had just left running towards me and not looking friendly at all, so of course I started to run hoping to not be eaten by this beast. Now I'm wearing platform shoes with an eight-inch heel which was fashionable in those days, but didn't help me run very fast so the dog finally caught up to me grabbing the windbreaker jacket I wore. Going through my mind was to escape at any cost so I got my arms out the jacket and ran into a nearby restaurant at the end of the block leaving the dog ripping the jacket apart. After regaining my composure, I ordered a drink from the restaurant to settle my nerves and made a call to the owners of the company letting them know that I had been attacked by a dog and needed to be picked up immediately. Their response was to continue to visit houses until our evening pickup, but that wasn't going to happen so I decided right then and there to quit and upon arriving at base camp that evening let them know of my decision. They told me that I couldn't stay in the motel that night so I had them drop me off at the local bus station where I spent the night until my dad wired me some money for a ticket to catch the bus back to Memphis the next morning. Filled with anger and disappointment I could hardly sleep thinking about my ordeal with that dog, plus sitting in a bus terminal in El Paso didn't help matters either, so basically I was catnapping until morning when my ticket was ready for the first bus headed for Memphis. On the bus ride my thoughts were of how angry my dad would be with me quitting my job but was stunned by his support as he again offered me a job with him and again, I told him that I didn't want to do that slave type work. Continuing with my job search around town I was almost in a state of depression about missing the opportunity to get to California, even tried partying with our friends but it didn't satisfy me. A short time after my return to Memphis got an offer that I couldn't refuse from the leader of the band that I had been a part of to come back to the band and go with them out to Los Angeles to audition for a spot on the Gong Show. Alas, now doors were opening up for me to pursue my dream of getting to California. I saw myself living as an adult and was determined to move forward with the idea of making it to California to pursue some of my dreams including music, art, football and bodybuilding. But before any of these dreams could happen there had to be a

Construction years as a Union Carpenter

lot of blood, sweat and tears put into perfecting our stage show before traveling to LA for a hopeful appearance on the Gong Show in Hollywood. Such as with sports, putting this band together was quite the adventure building some good chemistry but once we began to have regular daily practices and everyone started to vibe as one, we developed quite a presence as we performed in local night clubs to both help raise money for our trip and to put a little change in our pockets. Our shows usually were usually broken up into two acts, the opening list of songs followed by a short

Birth of a
VIOLATOR

intermission where we would change into different costumes for the second act sometimes wearing dresses, wigs and exotic scarfs and using a fog machine and special lighting to enhance the show like a few professional bands were doing in that era. If you missed the first show you might think you came to see the wrong band watching our second show because of the outrageous costumes. Some of our band members had regular jobs and families while some were still in school, so there was quite an eclectic group of musicians in our group. I had withdrawn from my sophomore year at Jackson State University where I majored in Art and performed in the marching band so to keep myself occupied most of the time when not practicing on my trumpet, I'd get these odd painting jobs doing murals in the high school, local night clubs, or someone's house. Life was pretty good in that regard, but my entire focus was on perfecting our show so we could make the trek to the West coast. During this period of time I got to know some of the business people in town on a professional level and saw kind of how they looked at things around the town and in Mississippi in general, none of which would convince me to stay and just exist when I had dreams of getting away to what I considered to be paradise to really spread my wings. I remember the crowds at our shows and how they connected with us, as I use to think to myself, I was born to do this. My brother was put in charge of watching the doors so that the night club owners couldn't screw us on the monies from the patrons coming to see our shows before we were taken to Memphis and was upset when I left to go back to the band. He had to finish high school and knew Dad wouldn't let him quit to follow me. There was another kid that we trusted to watch the money at the doors for us. We performed locally in night clubs for a few months before the band leader Ricky decided we were ready to make the trip to California to audition for a spot on the Gong Show. On the day of our departure I stopped by my mom's to say goodbye and just remembered how she resisted the idea of me leaving, saying that she didn't have any money to give me and that I was traveling so far from home and didn't know anyone in California. My response to her was that I'd been telling her that was where I wanted to go since high school and with the $27 dollars in my pocket, I'd get there and that I would know some people once I set foot there. She kissed me with tears in her eyes as I walked out of her house in July 1977 to pursue the next chapters of my life.

Chapter 3

Now the excitement has been kicked up a notch, we finally leave Mound Bayou in a van, two cars and a trailer to carry our equipment California bound with dreams of conquering the music world. Blasting the popular hit "Look at California", we were just focused on making a safe and enjoyable trip and taking in the sites as we drove across Interstate 10 heading west. As we entered each state the experiences became more exciting meeting new people and discovering a whole new world to most of us. The journey took about two and a half days to complete which did-n't bother anyone because we had a blast with each other along the ride. Taking turns driving and stopping just to take gas and bathroom breaks our caravan of the Brotherhood Convention moved closer and closer to our destination, I remember the whole thing feeling like we were on tour with it ending up on stage performing live at the Gong Show. That dream kept me filled with anticipation and that burning desire to be the best, ready to put the work in necessary to be successful. Once

Birth of a VIOLATOR

our caravan hit the California state line, we stopped just to celebrate completing the biggest part of the journey, taking pictures of the scenery with these plants we had only seen in books and watching westerns on the television. I was im-pressed by the beautiful landscape and mountains looking like they could touch the sky, even the cuisine we encountered along the way tasted much different than our usual southern cuisine. But I still couldn't wait to see those flowing palm trees like I'd seen watching the Rose Bowl games on television all those years and to walk along the beach and admire the Pacific Ocean up close. As we got closer to Los Angeles we took a wrong turn and ended up driving

My daughter

through the downtown area all the way down Broadway Street taking in the sights of people of almost every ethnicity conducting business, shopping, rustling and bustling along the sidewalks on both sides of the street until we jumped back on the Harbor freeway headed to the aunt and uncle's home of Ricky our band leader who lived in south central Los Angeles just off the corner of Main and El Segundo. It would be here where we lived and rehearsed our show that we would perform during the auditions for the Gong Show sometimes throwing a concert in their backyard. His uncle took a liking to me and would invite me out to his garage where he would enjoy smoking his pipe and telling me stories of how he'd left Mississippi and come to California and getting a factory job working nights. During the Watts riots in the 1960s he was often stopped by the police and questioned why he was out, so you had to carry a sticker showing that you were employed by the company and show your work schedule. Basically, he was sharing his wisdom with me maybe seeing something in me that reminded him of his younger days, I appreciate those conversations. I remember how the neighbors greeted us like we were members of their families, showing us how much respect they had for his aunt and uncle and the confidence that we had for ourselves driving all the way from Mississippi to take on such an endeavor to audition for such a show. It didn't take us long to begin to learn the city as we were always traveling back and forth to auditions in Hollywood plus our band leader had a sister who lived in the San Fernando valley where we spent a lot of time. Also, there were a lot of concerts in the park that we would enter just to further polish up our live performance and get some local publicity which wasn't hard because everyone already knew that we had to be from another region just by the way we dressed. Myself wore huge bell bottom pants with an 8" tall platform shoe, the same ones when running from the dog in El Paso, multi-colored shirts with the long collars, a fedora and rhinestone sunglasses. I was definitely into the whole Super Fly look, but the constant question we continually got was where did you guys come from?

Our answer was always that we came from the "Sip", which is what we called Mississippi. Even though they enjoyed busting our chops about the strange attire we wore, they enjoyed our music even more and it was almost like rooting for the underdog which we were looked at as especially coming from a small town in the South. July 4, 1977 holds a special place in my heart because that's the day we arrived in California and having achieved goal number one set my sights on accomplishing the rest of the goals and dreams on my list. The auditions we went through were very intense com-

My Son

peting against groups with all the latest and greatest musical equipment and fancy uniforms, looking down their noses at us like we were raggedy dolls and underestimating the hunger we had to succeed. But after all the bands we competed against had been eliminated, we got the final phone call to come into the studios in Hollywood to tape a live episode of the Gong Show. I guess it was destiny because we took first place on the show and got to meet some famous celebrity judges who were very impressed by our Funky sound. The band was a group of ten with a full horn section so our sound was powerful and we played all of the top hits for that era. We didn't have fancy uniforms or equipment but it never dampened our pride of what we represented and that was our hometown Mound Bayou, Mississippi. Guess we naturally had that underdog mentality because people were always judging us on our outward appearance, not ever breaking bread with us and really getting to know who we were but me personally still carry that chip on the shoulder and regardless of what you might think of me I continually attempt to let my light shine. After winning the grand prize on the Gong Show we were approached by several people from the music industry with all kinds of propositions for our band, and eventually we signed a contract with this producer who after us being around him and performing with one of his main artist for a while, occurred to us that he really wanted our horn section to add to the rhythm group he already had under contract. This began to put a strain on our personal relationships to the point of me getting kicked out of the band because I refused to go along with the idea of someone splitting us up just to fulfill his vision for his artist. So, it was at this point where performing wasn't the same, something had affected our chemistry to where you could feel our comradery fading away. After about a year of paying attorneys we were able to get out of our contract with this music producer, but by that time we'd missed out on the opportunity to be sponsored by Chuck, host of the Gong Show who wanted us to perform at his New Year's Eve party at his Hollywood home. After receiving a call from his secretary to come into the studio to play and he saw that the two trumpet players were missing, walked out of the audition and so went the opportunity to get introduced to the music industry executives who were going to attend his party. I had begun to set sights on my original goals to follow the dreams and visions I had back at home to make it to California, make a name for myself, get a good job, purchase a home, travel and enjoy the beauty of this country. Eventually our band the Brotherhood Convention broke up with some of the members going back to Mississippi but that thought never entered my mind as I got a job working at a garment manufacturing factory in Culver City, California making around $1.10 per hour. It wasn't much but I was doing what I had to do to survive here, pay my rent and not run back home. Before long I landed another job working nights at Los Angeles International Airport so the transit system became my best friend because there was just enough time between the factory job to grab a change of clothes and a snack before heading to the airport. Even the hurried schedules didn't bother me because inside was a fire burning to become successful and achieve as many of my dreams as I could so making wages became my main focus. As I continued to search the want ads, I landed a job at a McDonalds in Watts a subdivision of Los Angeles during the morning hours so I had to quit the job at the garment factory. The manager left an open invitation to come back if I ever needed a job, which was pretty classy to me but as time and experiences went on more opportunities came my way. After staying in a converted garage for a while, which part of would flood with any heavy rain plus you had to go inside our landlord's house to use the restroom and bath found a nice house to rent not far from the LA Coliseum on Hoover near 55th Street. The year was 1977 and after we got settled into the house I rented along with a few members from

Year 2 of the Violator

our band, started throwing big house parties and with the sound equipment we had made it seem like you were in a night club. The place was always packed with a female to male ratio of around five to one so the guys always had no problem grabbing a dance partner. Those parties were great, especially when my brother who was now in the military in Arizona or some old classmates who were also stationed at nearby military bases would stop by to say hello and indulge in the heavy card games that we played but it came to an abrupt end when people started crashing our parties and a friend of ours was assaulted just outside of a house during one of these parties. I spent most of my down time attending concerts to listen to some of the famous groups that we had patterned our style after with our band. I also competed in volleyball tournaments around the area just to stay fit and eventually purchased my first bench and weight set to workout at home. There were plenty of laughs and jokes about how I would never put on any substantial muscle, and if that didn't motivate me to make them eat their words nothing would. Just behind our house on the corner was a liquor store that was constantly being robbed and a lot of times the crooks would jump over the wall into our backyard to escape and my bedroom was at the rear of the house with no security bars on them, which prompted me to purchase my very first hand gun. I didn't intend to get caught slipping if someone decided to enter the house much to the dismay of my roommates, but I explained to them that I wasn't bringing a knife to a gunfight. We also got a Doberman Pinscher as an added deterrent but he scared our landlord as he galloped toward her when she stopped by to collect the rent and eventually gave us an ultimatum of getting rid of the dog or moving out because she often came by to check on things around the house. We ended up giving the dog to a friend who wanted him for breeding, but the whole fiasco caused us to look for another house. It was probably for the best because there was always some type of confrontations in that neighborhood with an occasional street fight or shootout. And for those who remember the religious worshippers that died in Guyana, one of our neighbors was included in that group. Her family had tried desperately to change her mind about making that trip but she was determined to go, the shock came when we heard her name called on the news. Still using the transit system, I went from my job at LAX

LA tailgating

to my day job with McDonalds for almost a year, still focused on reaching higher goals, obtaining better paying employment and hoping to eventually travel to Oakland, California to watch my favorite football team the Raiders. The manager at McDonalds eventually moved me up to assistant manager after working every position in the restaurant but still I searched for better paying jobs because I only made $1.90 per hour. Plus having to deal with the customers most who attended the high school down the street that would make a food purchase, eat most of their order then bring the rest back to the front counter complaining that something had been wrong with their order. This pissed me off every time it happened but the manager would instruct me to just redo the order and let them go on, not wanting any retaliation from the customers who some he knew had gang affiliations. The problem working two jobs is there wasn't much down time so my thinking was to find something to replace the wages I made from both jobs combined. Plus, I often got called in to work on my days off which I didn't like at all plus you couldn't wash the smell of burgers out of my clothes so there were stray dogs walking up to me following the scent of food while waiting on the bus. I got my first education on the gang situation in Los Angeles on one particular day while waiting to catch the bus home after picking up my check from work, as I was dressed in a black and red jogging suit with black and red shoes and this guy walks up to me and asked where I was from as he gave me the once over look. Telling him that I was from Mississippi was my pass because his message to me was that I had the wrong colors on for the area I was in and he advised me to not get caught in that part of town with these colors again because it just wasn't smart. As he walks away, I was so focused on the bus that I never gave much thought to what he had said until the next day at work. I told a co-worker what happened at the bus stop and he said brother you don't know how blessed you were because that incident could have ended a lot different for you. He went on to explain that wearing the wrong colors in the wrong area of town was good way to get stabbed, shot or worst and the guy who walked up to me had definitely given me a pass, as he showed me his blue bandana hanging out his back pocket. He went on to explain to me that the colors Blue and Red denoted certain gang affiliations and didn't mix together with good outcomes usually. From that day on I was constantly being aware of what colors to wear depending on the area I would be traveling, never taking Roy's advice for granted. One day at work while taking my break the security guard told me about some opportunities in the construction industry where they needed minorities to fill up so many positions, he said to me that he could see that I was getting burnt out with the situation there because I was only getting paid $1.90 per hour and even being called in to work on my days off intensified the thoughts of moving on to something more substantial. So I took a sick day and met with this guy the security guard had directed me to go see in Downtown Los Angeles not sure of what I was getting into. The meeting went very well and at the conclusion the guy asked me to pick one of the construction fields listed on the paper and I remembered how my dad wanted my brother and I to work with him in the construction industry. My attitude back then was that was slave work after trying it over a summer and promised him it wasn't for me. Here comes the same opportunity again, but didn't seem quite as bad as I'd remembered when my dad tried to get me into the building trades. This guy I met with was the conduit to get a union job in the industry and after explaining to me that my starting wages would be $3.11 per hour, I picked out a company that I thought made sound equipment which would have kept me near the music industry. Now he informs me of the fees it took to sign up with the union which at that time was $250 so as I started to get up and leave his office he says to me, son I don't want you to miss this opportunity to get in the union, make some decent money with health benefits and a retirement. He ask me to sit back down and takes out this huge checkbook from his desk, fills out a check and gives it to me and tells me to go see another guy he called 'Red' across town at the Carpenters local #1506, give him this check and get enrolled in the union. Now mind you I'm thinking to myself is this guy some kind of loan shark so I asked him, how am I supposed to pay your money back and he said worry about that after you get enrolled into the union apprenticeship program and get a job. Feeling pretty nervous as I drove across town to Santa Monica Blvd. in Hollywood and the address he'd given to me, went in spoke with this guy 'Red' who was seated at a long table looking like one of those mob bosses you'd see on television. He welcomed me inside took a quick look at the check I gave him and said to me, welcome to the brotherhood. He instructed me to see the secretary to get enrolled in the Carpenters union. I also was immediately enrolled in their apprenticeship program and had to attend night classes for two years before graduating and becoming a journeyman with a starting salary of $11.37 per hour. Going back to my previous jobs to inform both bosses that I would be moving on was pretty exciting for me because I felt in my spirit that better days were ahead, especially when some guy who I had never met me before filling out a personal check of his for me to get into this union. In regards to me referring to my guardian angels, this seemed to be another one of those occasions. Again, as with moving on from my factory job, both bosses wished me well and left an open invitation to return if necessary. Now was the task of purchasing all of the tools on a list I got from the Union Hall and was familiar with a few of them from working with my dad, others left me wondering what the hell they were to be used for plus I had to buy a pair of work boots and other related clothing. That ended up costing around $150 and I'm questioning my decision but went in for the interview with this company that hired me in Glendale, California where the owner greeted me, introduced me to my supervisor, asked if I was ready to go to work as I stood there wearing my long Geri curl and new stiff work boots and assured him that I was ready. He gave me an address to the jobsite for me to report to the next day. Mind you now, I'm thinking that I'll be building music speakers and sound equipment so when I reached the address couldn't believe that it was the GM plant in Van Nuys, California. We had to use a Thomas guide for directions back then in 1978 and I was convinced that the address had to be wrong, so cruising around the area looking for what I thought should have been where he must have meant for me to go made me late for my first day and I got reamed out by the foreman who had been waiting for me since 6:00 a.m. I finally arrived on the jobsite about 6:45 a.m. which could've been my first and last day on that site. Guess you could say it was a rocky beginning and through my whole confusion as to where the sound equipment and speakers were, the foreman reassured me that the next time I came in late to just go back to the office. Neither did it sound good, but it meant you might get let go because there was very little tolerance for tardiness, or not having the proper tools for the job. He needed me there to help him install these heavy panels on the walls to absorb some of the noise inside the factory. Suddenly I'm feeling the pressure of catching on with the work as quick as possible and never arriving late again, which didn't take long to get adapted to. Funny thing is, I was so nervous about arriving late to the job that I left my lights on to my pinto and upon finishing work for the day had to ask my foreman to jump-start my battery which had run down. So my journey takes off with a bang, work was so plentiful that I never missed any time and ended up putting in a lot of overtime which was great because I could pay back the guy who gave me my union initiation check and my only bills at that time were my car payment and rent. I can remember some of my duties as an apprentice were mostly loading materials on jobsites, unloading supply trucks and box cars of trains, trashing out jobsites, hand-screwing hanger wires with a contraption made out of a metal pole and a crank attached to one end of it with another tube duct taped to it to hold my wires for suspending the ceilings. Talk about some back breaking and physically taxing work, but I never complained because that wasn't going to be the reason I got laid off. I was totally focused on being the best apprentice that I could be under the circumstances, being the only black guy in the company and the ridicule that came with that mainly had my mind on my money which was quite a significant raise from my days working at McDonald's and LAX airport. Getting use to the dirt and grime was just part of my adjustment to the construction industry, somedays I had to bring a change of clothes to drive home in because I didn't want to ruin the interior of my Ford pinto which I kept immaculate. I also started wearing a baseball cap trying to keep the dust out of my hair which was almost impossible especially wearing a Geri curl which dust was drawn to like a magnet. I remembered what my parents had told me about getting a car when I was in high school, they both said when you pay for your vehicle you'll appreciate it more than if we bought it for you and believe me when I say that my appreciation of that car was real. Think about traveling on the local transit system carrying my tools in a five-gallon bucket to driving to all the different locations I was sent to work around Southern California. So yes, till this day my appreciation for owning a vehicle hasn't faded one bit. As time went on my employer suggested that I get a truck if I intended to stay employed because they wanted the employees to carry work materials from the office, or pick up certain supplies from the warehouses we did business with. Here again I'm feeling the pressure to try and trade in my pinto for a pickup and finding a dealership that would work with me to make this happen, so after checking around there was a dealership who agreed to take my pinto in trade. Even with the trade value the only vehicle that I could really afford was a cargo van which I had driven before back in Mississippi and fell in love with, so I showed up to work driving my new van and the boss and co-workers got quite a laugh out of my assertiveness to keep my job and now I could carry a lot more materials than before that would scratch up the inside of my car. The van had metal across the back windows and the guys had a running joke that I hoisted televisions at night. But with all of the adjustments, work was great because now I'm being sent to bigger jobs farther away than I'd ever imagined and stayed constantly busy because I was cheap labor. I continued to attend apprenticeship school at night. During this time, I began to lift weights to better prepare my body for the rigors that I faced because failing wasn't an option for me and the job duties assigned to me was heavy lifting, loading and stocking the jobsites. A year or so later I got into bodybuilding as a way to really challenge myself to keep getting bigger and stronger. Looking back to my days in high school, I remember loving that pumped feeling from doing calisthenics so it was like walking down memory lane and soon was bitten by the competitive bug and began to compete in bodybuilding contests. My co-workers use to always ask me what I had been doing as they saw my physique changing and all I would say to them was that I was eating lots of chicken and doing pushups because I didn't know what they thought about the whole bodybuilding life-style I was into. There was one other guy who worked at the company that lifted weights at his local gym and I thought that we would become good friends but it didn't happen. Rumor was that he took some of my new tools out of my bucket and exchanged them with some old ones as part of my initiation. I never found out which co-worker actually stole my tools and after that started to color code and engrave them, so if anyone ever got any tools without my permission there would be hell to pay. A few of the younger co-workers came to some of my competitions to support me but for the most part there was a lot of teasing about me looking muscle-bound and all that did was strengthen my resolve to push forward, just knowing how much it irritated them the more pleasure I got from being dedicated to the art of bodybuilding. As my commitment grew so did my clothes sizes, which just inspired me even more because I could appreciate the whole process of working hard, playing hard and feeling like my life was moving in a positive direction. As fate would have it there was a friend of mine who became my custom tailor and made any outfit that I'd design for him, the guy was really gifted with needle and thread so most of my casual and dressy attire was all custom made for me. The hardest part about that was giving the clothes away I'd outgrown so mostly they were donated to Goodwill, but my growth kept me pushing to see how far I could take this new passion. My competitive career began in 1981 and ended in 1989, during that time I competed about five to six times per year as not to burn myself out and competed natural which took lots of hard work, dedication and focus but the rewards were price-less just knowing I was going head to head with guys who were using steroids and holding my own on stage. For me, the real competition was with myself to put the necessary work in to push my body as close to what I'd envisioned as humanly possible and the true joy was with the barbells and dumb bells as your tools of the trade you and you alone become sort of a Michael Angelo with your own body. My highest ranking was a second place finish in my class of the Mr. Los Angeles contest in 1984. Through my years of bodybuilding I met quite a few people who honed their crafts and took their physiques to the next level to compete on the pro circuit, also got to meet some of the best professional bodybuilders in the game. Some of the best advice given to me during those years of training was from one of the members of my gym named James who just happened to be a youth gang counselor. He always told me to remember that I was in the sport to become a bodybuilder, not a powerlifter and to use the weights as a tool to chisel your physique into the masterpiece you visualize for you. He also advised me to remain natural so that twenty years down the road I could still be able to play with my grandkids, educating me on some of the dangers of steroid usage which I'm forever grateful. He had won many trophies during his competitive days and he wasn't a big guy but so shredded. I looked at him taking me under his wing as another one of those guardian angels sent to guide me through those moments. As my quest to mold myself into this superhero I'd seen myself as since childhood, the workouts became like a therapy session combining a one mind, body and spirit mentality every time I trained. Balancing work, training and family life took every fiber in me and looking back on it I wouldn't have changed a thing. Just going through the rituals of preparing for the competitions pushed me to limits unthinkable as it was usually six to eight weeks of strict eating especially as a contest approached and the specific training depending on what area of my body I needed to focus on at that particular time plus still performing my duties at work. The rewards of these Spartan rituals were presenting a polished physique on stage oiled up and wearing only posing trunks to show the efforts of all my hard work, being satisfied with the present package but always striving to be better the next time on stage. I placed well in some contest and not so well in others, but at the end of the day am thankful for the opportunities, the people and the memories from the sport and still to this day keep some type of physical activity in my everyday life because the "bug" that I had years ago when I first picked up a barbell is still inside of me. After finally moving out of our rental on 55th street I moved the family to Baldwin Park, California which was about a forty minute drive east of Los Angeles into a beautiful condominium but only stayed there about a year because one of my co-workers in construction named Steve would always come over and toss a hand full of money out of my upstairs window to paint the picture for me that renting was just throwing my money out the same way. He would say to me, Wayne you're making the same wages as I am so I'm pushing you to cross that threshold and purchase a home like he had done. He had a beautiful house in Diamond Bar, California not far from my condo so I started putting money aside to start looking for a home to purchase. He and I used to do a lot of side jobs which were plentiful at that time so I was able to stack up my money pretty fast. Steve and I met on a project in the twin towers Downtown Los Angeles installing ceilings striking a good friendship lasting even after he moved to Florida after his divorce. In the meantime, I ended my lease at the condo and moved in with a couple of my friends from the band in Los Angeles near 67th and Figueroa where I stayed until the time, I finally saved up enough to go house hunting. During my stay there with them we remodeled the house which gave me plenty of experience that was used further down the road. Also during that time, the Raiders had moved to Los Angeles from Oakland which was like Christmas in July, so I started attending the games at the Coliseum sometimes alone but all I knew was I was finally getting a chance to see my favorite team since childhood in person. I would take the city transit to the games so I didn't have to deal with parking, plus it was a straight shot up Figueroa to the stadium. Soon after most of my wardrobe was Raiders gear and to me this was just another piece of living the dream. Leaving a jobsite at the Veterans Hospital one afternoon in the San Fernando Valley I was hit broadside by a city truck pulling a tree trimmer and at the time wasn't wearing my seatbelt which caused me to be thrown to the passenger side of the van and knocked out cold. Upon regaining consciousness my head was underneath the dashboard and feet up in the passenger seat, I must have suffered a concussion because there were yellow birds flying around my head. By the time the driver of the truck had pulled over to the side and made it to my van all I could do was stare out the passenger side window and wonder why the kids walking by coming home from school were pointing at the van. Once he helped me to my feet and asked if I was okay and I replied yes, he knew that I was in shock but I didn't want to wait for any medical services or the police. My mind was on getting home so I wouldn't miss work the next day. I didn't realize that the force of the collision had ruptured my gas tank and caved in the entire left side of the van just behind the driver's door until walking around to that side of it. I insisted on driving all the way from the Valley to where I was living in South Central LA leaking fuel the whole way. My guardian angel was definitely with me on that day and the following day I was in so much pain that I couldn't even sit up and swore to never ride in a vehicle without wearing a seatbelt. I made a call to my boss Richard to let him know about the accident on yesterday and I needed to take my van to a repair shop and he told me to just let him know when I was able to get back to work. I drove the van to the dealership where I'd purchased it and there was no damage to the frame so what they did was take half of another van's body and welded it to the undamaged side. Meantime I went to get checked out by a doctor and picked up some pain medication and stiches for the lacerations to my head. After driving a rental for about a month my van was repaired and looked good as new so I was back in the saddle and off and running. My prayers were answered in 1984 when the dream became reality as I was able to purchase a duplex on Mullen Street and Slauson Avenue in West Los Angeles and quickly began my lessons in both homeownership and being a landlord because part of the agreement between the seller and I was that her dad who lived in one side of the duplex remain as my tenant. It was a small place square footage wise but that took nothing away from the feeling of accomplishment I felt at actually owning my first house, being able to put my signature on the property. The first thing that made me feel some pressure in the neighborhood was one of the elders who lived across the street came over, introduced himself, welcomed me and almost immediately began to ask when I expected to put some paint on the house. I knew right then that there was a lot of pride of ownership in the neighborhood and quickly let him know that I too was happy to have gotten the property and would definitely add my personal touches to it as time and money permitted. What was really nice about my duplex was the long driveway which afforded plenty of parking and had a garage so I could store some of my tools for work. Looking back, I think the elders were checking me out because I was probably one of the youngest homeowners on that street which was predominately retirees and wanted to get a feel for me. They would tell me that they knew when I was going to work because of my loud music blasting in my van at 4:00 in the morning. Life was good, work was good, training was good and then my first tenant began playing dodgeball with me when the rent was due which didn't set well with me at all, but one of my first lessons was quickly learning how to legally deal with this type of situation. As time

NFL Hall of Fame parade in 2000

moved on I ended up evicting my tenant and quickly remodeled the unit so it could be rented again, which took a while with me only getting a few hours after work each day to try and finish everything that needed to be repaired so I got help from a few friends. Upon finishing the unit, I rented it to a young couple with two small kids. Things went great in the beginning with my new tenants but just as before the dodgeball game was on again. This time around using the knowledge I'd retained from before and giving fair opportunities to get the rent paid had to evict them also. I felt sorry for them because they lived across the street before in the wife's mother's house and thinking of helping them move right across the street to stay near family with the kids they had, they instead spit in my face by not honoring the rental agreement. After trying to add on to the property with no success because of mounting cost of permits and construction, I began to look for another property to buy because by now my family is outgrowing where we lived with the birth of my second child. During this time as I'm traveling along the 405-freeway heading north to a jobsite in the city of Calabasas, still dark outside something struck my windshield and completely shattered my dash sending my stereo against the rear doors. I swerved in front of a tractor trailer truck trying to pull off the road to get out of the van because in my mind it was going to explode any second. After getting out and running to the nearest call box on the side of the freeway, I kept waiting for the explosion that never happened and when a Highway Patrol pulled up to me on his motorcycle he started laughing. He pointed at my face and when I went to touch it, he grabbed my hands and said that my face looked like a porcupine because of the shards of glass embedded in my face. He said that my glasses saved my eyes from being punctured and called for an ambulance that took me to UCLA hospital emergency room to get the glass removed from my face. The reasons I didn't feel the glass in my face was the shock I was in plus it was a cold winter morning.

Needless to say when the dealership that had fixed this same van before took a look at it when I had it towed back to them, they said it was totaled because the tire that had fallen from another vehicle on the other side of the freeway, bounced up and hit my windshield peeling the roof back like a tuna can. They informed me that to repair it would take putting a completely new roof on the van and wished me luck in purchasing another vehicle. After waiting for my insurance to issue a check I started car shopping once again, this time only being able to purchase another van because trucks were sold at a premium and I couldn't afford them. I ended up getting another van just like the last but with a more luxurious interior, almost too nice to work out of but soon I was back on the road. I had my huge speaker box installed so I had my music like before that my neighbors told me was like an alarm clock to them when I left home heading to work around 4:00 a.m.. Still needing to find a larger home, one of my co-workers told me about this new housing track out in Rancho Cucamonga where he had recently purchased a home. With the work that we did you had to travel all over anyway so I said to him what the hell I'll take a look at the area and the houses. I drove out to hopefully get a lottery number for building a house in that phase and was fortunate to do so. Soon after getting all the documentations in place I bought my second house in Rancho Cucamonga, thus beginning a new chapter of my journey. We moved into the house in 1990, quickly getting settled in, getting my two kids Demetria and Orlando Jr. situated with school and getting acquainted with this ever-growing community. During the late eighties and early nineties the construction industry was going through some rough times, so to keep a steady paycheck coming in I had to work out of town for a while, which was an adventure in itself living out of a suitcase, eating out every night, hanging out at bars which cost extra, plus dealing with motels and the likes. We landed a big store project in Porterville, California which lasted about three months so no way we were trying to drive the three hours it took to get there every day. There was this hard-nosed superintendent who threatened to kick me off his project because I never wore shirts with any sleeves on the job. And the fact that I had this huge Raiders flag hanging from my scissor lift and I wore my hard hat backwards drove him nuts. Our arguments continued for weeks until he demanded that I cover my shoulders up, so I took two pieces

44

of cardboard and attached them to my sleeveless shirt with duct tape. Then came the deal with my hard hat, and by then he had me so pissed that I took the webbing out of my hat, punched holes on each side and made a chin strap out of ceiling wire and duct tape allowing the hat to sit on top of my glasses which really pissed him off. The guys on my crew saw that he was picking on me because I was the only black person on the jobsite and stood with me through the ordeal. Eventually I went to a local store and bought some t-shirts to wear, but my hard hat and my flag remained for the duration of the project. Through the will to succeed I pushed on making the best of my job situation always praying for better days when I didn't have to work out of town and could enjoy the comforts of my home, but with our economy being on a decline the construction industry continued to suffer and the bigger jobs became harder to get. In 1996 while working on a project down in the shaft of an elevator installing drywall, injured my back and had to be off work for six weeks. After completing my rehab and getting released to go back to work, I was told by my superintendent that the company was heading in a different direction and laid me off. I went to my union hall to file a grievance against the company and basically was told that it would be hard to prove unlawful termination unless I had witnesses. Feeling like I was getting the run around took my complaint to the labor board and after looking over my case ruled in my favor, leaving no chance of ever working for that company again after being there eighteen years. Here's when I stared to experience missing lots of work hours because I wasn't known outside of the company I had just sued, so it was hard to gain employment especially when I stated to other companies that I had been employed for eighteen years with one contractor, they suddenly pictured me as an older guy who must have been slow. I would hear from them, we'll get back to you which meant that they weren't going to hire me and immediately started thinking of other avenues to make extra cash, even to the point of working with non-union companies and dealing with the on-going war between the Carpenters union and these non-union outfits. Many times, getting followed by union stewards from the supply warehouses to the jobsites as they searched for these non-union contractors to pressure into signing on with union because they had been taking a bite out of the union industry for years. On several occasions I got busted working non-union jobs and my answer to the stewards was, you'd rather catch me working here on these jobsites than coming through your window in a ski-mask because I'm going to find a way to feed my kids and keep my house. I was labelled a "Renegade" and after being caught several times working with non-union contractors was suspended from the union for about six months or so, long enough to lose my medical coverage and with two small kids one trip to the hospital could have been devastating, but I kept my head up through the whole deal and eventually was re-instated back into the union having to go before the board and take an oath to remain loyal to the brotherhood. In the back of my mind I'm thinking that the union wasn't loyal to me by not honestly searching for employment opportunities for me or standing behind any grievances I may have had, but swore my allegiance to get back on board. So, I began bouncing around from company to company trying to hopefully find a home which was very hard with companies trying to hold on to their main employees. That part was the toughest because you were quickly labeled a "Floater" meaning you were the last one hired and the first one fired when work slowed down plus for me it was mostly the case where I had no relatives in the industry so even though I worked my butt off was still one of the first to be floated out. I began to wonder if I'd be able to survive in construction for the thirty years it took before you could retire with a full pension. I'm very thankful to those who encouraged me to tough it out and keep my mind on my pension when everything looked hopeless, because by now I was vested with the union and shouldn't throw those years out the window. Even with their encouraging words I still went through that pattern of floating from company to company, when and wherever employment could be acquired. One particular non-union job I worked on repairing the ceilings in a grocery store, took a fall through the scaffolding when the planks broke. Quickly grabbing another plank to keep from hitting the floor fourteen feet below, I bruised my ribs and had to go to the clinic the contractor told me to visit. Taking a couple of days to recover I looked for employment elsewhere and never went back to the project. I truly believe that I've been protected by guardian angels along this journey of mine, for instance this particular jobsite I was working on where the tapers got a kick out of leaving their taping mud all over the floor and splattering the back of my clothes with mud that they flicked my way. My foreman took notice of their actions and asked them to try and keep the areas cleaner where I was dragging a 100-foot power cord attached to a screw pole installing hanger wires for our ceilings. They laughed and told him to mind his business so the following morning while everyone's having their coffee, he told me to take a walk with him inside the building. Now I'm curious as to what he wants to show me, so he walks over to where the tapers kept their mud covered, pulls off the coverings and took some small packets from his pocket. It was relatively dark inside except for the string of lights hung along the site, but I just remember hearing him tear open these packets and sprinkling the contents into the mud and stirring everything up. Never saying a word to me, he covers up the mud and goes back out to his truck and finishes having coffee and I sit back in my car until it was time to clock in for work. During the day my foreman still never spoke about what he'd done earlier but I noticed him watching the tapers with interest as they spread their joint mud on the newly installed walls. They continued with their usual pranks flicking mud and leaving the floors a mess, so when we took a lunch break, I tried to inquire as to what happened earlier that morning when he asked me to accompany him inside the building but all he said was just wait. After completing our work for the day and locking up our work chest we both leave the jobsite. Now here's where things got interesting the next morning as everyone begins their workday, we could hear the tapers talking among themselves trying to figure out why the walls were covered with these yellow spots. My foreman and I kept working on the ceilings but I swear I could almost see a grin on his face as we listened to the tapers chattering about the spots on the wall because they were spreading to the point the wall looked like a leopard. Eventually they added another coat of mud on the walls in hopes of fixing the issue with the spots, but the next day to their amazement the spots not only had bled through that new layer of mud but also had grown larger than yesterday. Their foreman decided to cover up the entire area with a paint product called Kilz in hopes of preventing a repeat of the previous day, but the next day the yellow spots were still present and even larger. A representative from the taper's office stopped by the jobsite to see what the fuss was about these spots all over the walls, and upon seeing the walls instructed them to take off the drywall down to the studs and start over. The superintendent running the project wasn't happy with them having to reinstall the drywall, so he had them score the wall board just below our ceiling line so that we could continue to install the ceiling grid which made another joint to be taped just below our finished ceiling. The tapers were so focused on fixing their dilemma that they never bothered me again and I never saw or worked with that foreman again the rest of my career in construction. I later found out that what my foreman had sprinkled into the taping mud was mustard seeds, which took me back to something my mom spoke about having faith the size of a mustard seed and all you needed to do was plant it, wet it and watch it grow. To me this foreman was another guardian angel I encountered along my journey.

Chapter 4

As stated previously, my love for the game of football was very strong and began to be therapeutic during the ups and downs of my work, family and life in general. I remember going to my first Raiders game at the LA Coliseum, standing at the historic peristyle entrance staring at the field and reminding myself of my dream of watching them play in person and that dreams do come true if you believe and continually pursue them. Just the pure excitement of game day made me temporarily forget about any issues I had in life for the entire day, and depending on the outcome of the games, that excitement would carry me into a state of euphoria or send me into a state of depression lasting long after the game was over. Even going back to work sometimes I performed my duties in a virtual fog, especially after losing to a divisional opponent which was the worst because we faced them twice a season so you at least hoped to split victories for playoff implications. I'm a "DIE-HARD" Raiders fan who's been told more often than not that I take the game too seriously, but how else should we the fans who spend our hard-earned dollars to come out and support the team we love take this game. After a few years of watching my team in person, I felt like something was missing, something to really get the home crowd engaged into the game because some fans were too cool for school and use to always question why I stood up and was so loud all the time. I would remind them that we were at a football game and even though people were caught up in the whole Hollywood scene, this was a place to make some noise and inspire the team. So, the season home opener in 1991 I along with a few friends came up with costumes that we would wear with our faces streaked with "War-paint" and in my case spiked shoulder pads to express the intensity I felt on game day and called ourselves 'The Enforcers'. That year my character the "Violator" was released into society and the reception spanned both ends of the spectrum as fans looked on in amazement as we'd walk around the stadium parking lots getting the fans pumped up before we took our passion and intensity inside the arena and there were some who wouldn't let their kids get near us. The kids looked at us like living cartoon characters and just wanted to hang out with us, which felt strange at first but we quickly adjusted and the parents started to change the way they had perceived us earlier. Soon part of the game day ritual was taking photos with as many fans as possible. I think it began a new era in LA which lacked a bit when it came to being loud and vocal during those critical moments in the game where I felt our crowd noise could make a difference, possibly changing momentum for our team's advantage. I took a windshield shade and made a huge sign that read "GET LOUD" on one side and "We're here to PUMP you up!" on the other and I'd stomp up and down the bleachers in an attempt to get our fans pumped up and emotionally into the battles on the playing field. As large as the Coliseum is, when everyone participated the stadium noise was deafening and our defense fed off of it. I would leave the stadium exhausted from the energy spent hyping the crowd at every game but wouldn't change any of it, thus I call it "Therapy". The friends and families I met over the next twenty-nine years from around the world and the memories are absolutely priceless. If not for the "Violator" character, I don't think the experience would've been the same. As I stomped around the parking lots at the Los Angeles Coliseum people would share their food and drinks with me and at times would be walking around with several beers in my hands not being able to finish them before I was given more. This made it difficult to shake hands and greet the fans until one particular Sunday I met this gentleman with a strong Kentuckian accent who was playing dominoes with a group of guys at their tailgate. His name was 'Raider' Ron Rickard and one of his friends suggested of me to trade those beers for one cup of liquor so I could travel light and wouldn't spend most of the game standing in line at the restrooms like I had been doing before, missing a lot of the game. He told me that it would be better to drink quality over quantity and ever since brown liquor became an intricate part of my game day rituals. Ron and I hit it off from the beginning because of his passion for the team and his sense of humor and over the years became great friends. He and I even went on a road trip to Oakland for a game after the team moved back where my stepsons rode along with us. It was quite the experience and we remained close friends until he passed away where his wife Janet asked me to speak at his home going service attended by Raiders team vice president Marc Badain and his wife. Ron and Marc had been friends for quite a while but I don't think that Marc knew how close Ron and I were until that day. Rest in paradise brother, gone but never forgotten. Each year I kept refining my costume constantly approaching the look I'd had in my mind of how I wanted to appear at the games, going through several boot styles, several pants styles, a few different shoulder pads, different spike combinations, different jerseys and designing the look for my face paint which was applied with two fingers in the beginning until I began using art brushes for a cleaner more detailed look. I remember the first game, walking down to my seat and a cameraman for the NFL called me over to where he was changing film to ask where I was sitting. After showing him the spot, he said that they would be getting some footage, because no one was dressing in this manner, especially in Los Angeles at that time. A short time later I saw my screaming face on the opening monologue of a nationally televised sports show Inside the NFL, where I sent an autographed photo to the producer Steve Sabol who posted it in the building's lobby and wrote me letter commending me for the look and the energy I brought to the games. Eventually some of the media forums started doing interviews wanting to know why I dressed in this manner for the games, I told them about my passion for the game and thus my attire was just an expression of said passion and that I intended to show up at every game in my "Violator" attire. One of my most memorable moments in Los Angeles was being given a note during a game by security from the team's front office to meet them at their postgame dinner at a nearby hotel. Thinking I'd done something to upset them temporarily kind of distracted my attention from the game but had to put those thoughts aside and focus on the battle raging on the field. In the note I had been instructed to take the paint off my face so they could see who I was, so after arriving at the team's hotel I wiped as much of the paint as possible from my face and reluctantly made my way toward the room where they were having postgame dinner. I ran into several players who were making their way upstairs and they're telling me that this was the right place and they were waiting on me which put a lump in my throat thinking to myself, this can't be good, but how wrong I was. After

My Brothers:
Toozak & Gorilla Rilla

grabbing a plate of food, I was shown to my table which consisted of some of the top executives and their families who welcomed me to sit and join them as they introduced me to everyone and also wanted to know the person making all the noise in the Pirate's Pavilion, which was the metal bleaches in the east end zone. Finally figuring out that I wasn't in trouble I started to explain to them about my mission to help the fans better enjoy their experience when attending our games, how we could influence the momentum of the game and feel more connected to the team. I looked at us as warriors in the stands, rooting our team on to victory just like the gladiators in the arenas of battle throughout history. So as it turned out this meeting was the beginning of a long relationship that's still going today. I also got to meet some players and their families up close and quite a few said they liked what I was doing to get the home crowd revved up during the games and they did feed off the energy in the stadium, they encouraged me to continue with my mission. My drive home after that dinner was a blur because of all the thoughts going through my mind as to what was really behind what had just taken place, but couldn't wait to get back to work so I could prepare for the next home game. Feeling like I'd gotten the King's blessing shifted into high gear interacting with the opposing fans as well to share the good times that game day brought as we tailgated all around the stadium. It's always been more like fellowshipping with the fans in my mind, leaving the battles to the gridiron. By this time both my daughter and son were old enough to attend the games with me which was awesome because I saw it as a family affair type of experience and having them there to witness the events at a young age was my way of starting our family tradition as Raiders fans. We had our front row seats in the east end zone named the Pirate's Pavilion where it was our custom to stand for the entire game, keeping that energy flowing with the fans and having a blast the whole day. They donned their game day attire along with me as we made the early morning drive from Rancho Cucamonga around 6:00 a.m. to get our spot in line waiting for the gates to open so we could begin our tailgate rituals, fellowshipping with other families before game time. There were a few families who would watch and feed my kids as my buddies and I stomped around the parking lots meeting and greeting all in attendance kind of like an ambassador for the team, but it just felt good meeting people from all over the world most whom I probably wouldn't have had the opportunity were it not for my outrageous attire, so one of my favorite sayings is "never judge a book by its cover". Again, I say thank you to those families that watched and fed my kids in Lot 6 of the coliseum. My journey felt like it was moving in a positive direction, inspiring me to continue my game day rituals and hopefully enhancing everyone's experience that I ran into. There was never a dull moment during the years at the LA Coliseum because if it wasn't some of our fans giving the visiting fans a hard time, or watching law enforcement breaking up fights in the stands which I never understood, sometimes even home fans fighting home fans which blew my mind. There was couple I knew who were both police officers who told me that they enjoyed working at the LA Coliseum because they were making overtime, could watch the game for free and handle the unruly fans. I always thought that we were stronger together and felt like the visiting fans should have been treated better. I remember my first postgame interview with Glen Walker who was a sports reporter and that opened the doors to many more inquiring interviews. It was there at the Coliseum where I met Gloria and Gabe who traveled down from Oakland and we became great friends and this young kid fresh out of the Marines named Sean Camacho who said to me, one day I'm going to dress up like that for the games. Who knew just a few years later we would meet again in Oakland with him portraying his character 'Senor Raider'? Those thirteen years in Los Angeles were full of highs and lows, but over-

Toozak, Raider Ron & VIOLATOR

all, the memories are priceless and in 1995 after years of failed negotiations with the LA Coliseum commission the team moved back to Oakland. Talk about going into a total depression, was the state of mind I was in wondering how they could just leave us overnight. While hearing the news on television and receiving calls from friends my thoughts were how was I going to firstly get tickets in Oakland and keep the same seats I'd had in Los Angeles, and secondly how to make the trips up to Oakland after hearing about the whole PSL fee which was way above my pay grade at the time. Fortunately my employer at that time was a huge Raiders fan also and I figured I'd ask him for a loan to cover my PSL and arranged to pay off the loan which he agreed to, next I started writing letters trying to explain my dilemma as far as the tickets were concerned. To my surprise I got a response from an Oakland Coliseum executive who advised me he knew who I was from seeing me on television and to be sure and get my monies in before the deadline, which I did and anxiously waited to get my tickets in the mail having no idea where my seat would be. Unknown to me during this transitional period, there was a lot of tension building up at home because of my going up to Oakland for the games, which I started to sense but for the most part ignored because of my passion for the team. I hooked up with a friend who I'd met in LA who was also getting tickets in Oakland so we would often make the trips together grabbing flights from LAX or Burbank on Southwest airlines fully dressed in our game day attire which took on a life of its own again because no one else was dressing in this manner, let alone flying on planes. Sometimes the flight attendants would ask us to serve the snacks during the flights, much to the delight of the passengers. Taking pictures with the flight crew and passengers made those trips feel like a hop skip and a jump because by the time the party on the plane got good it was time for us to land. There were a lot of media personnel from Los Angeles going up for the games plus the team's cheerleaders for a while until they decided to hire a new group, so we got to know them quite well over the next couple of years. I had the pleasure of meeting the parents of team executive Amy Trask who I'd met when the Raiders moved to Los Angeles at their training facilities in El Segundo where often she would stop by to say hello and ask why I was there. My answer was just to be close to my team since I had a day off work. I loved the fact that she never belittled me for sitting outside of the facility. They treated me like part of the family and I enjoyed our conversations during those flights to Oakland. Upon arrival to the airport I would always check to see if they needed anything before taking off to the stadium. On the first flight into Oakland a buddy Tim and I were going to walk to the stadium but were picked up by the parents of Mike Pickett who told us to jump into their truck because they knew by the way we were dressed that we were headed to the game. I remember his sister sandwiched between us in the back seat and wondered what she thought about her dad picking up two absolute strangers dressed like a couple of Nomad warriors. They own the company 'Cytosport' that makes Muscle Milk and other nutritional products, we still remain friends today and they would invite Bertha and I up to their suite at the stadium. I would meet and greet everyone in their suite and enjoy some of the catered food and beverages, but would only stay for a short time because I didn't want to scare their guest by going crazy while the game was being played because it was hard to not get emotional like when I'm down in the hole with my rowdy friends. Though the trips to and from the games left little sleep time I never missed a work day because of making my trips to the games, even when the outcome was unfavorable. Just the fact that I could still attend the games in person kept me striving to do whatever was necessary to continue making these trips. Most of my co-workers couldn't believe that I was so passionate about the team to put myself through the rigors of the trips and never taking a day off before coming back to work. My response to them was that it's what I felt I had to do and had the responsibility of reporting to work on time to make my money. They couldn't see it from my perspective of how I was making my dreams become reality and each experience kept me inspired to push forward because there were plenty visions and dreams that I had in mind to accomplish along my journey. One of those dreams inspired by Coach John Madden was to get myself a custom motorhome for traveling to the games both in Oakland and other stadiums around the country. He had his personal driver but I want to drive my own rig. Two of my favorites are the Renegade and Showhauler motorhomes because of the diesel truck cab which lends a different level of safety, plus it reminds me of the cement trucks my dad let me drive as a kid. I'm still pursuing this custom RV for my football road trips across the country and hopefully will find the right dealership to make it happen. Bertha and I got invited to Cheryl's famous treehouse in the hills of East Oakland where we met her family and a few friends and just enjoyed the hospitality that evening before a Raiders game. Soon after came media request to make appearances on different network shows, where they would come to me or I would show up in my "Violator" attire to their studios just as I'd been told by one well known Hall of Fame Raiders player Howie back at that postgame meal in LA. Then came numerous newspaper editorials who did articles about the team's move back to Oakland and usually my face was used somewhere in the articles, which I looked at as positive progression and over the years established a friendly relationship with quite a few media personalities. On top of that, commercial opportunities came along which further added to my character's exposure and feeding the lore that was surrounding this fanatical fan with the zebra-striped face and spiked shoulder pads. Through all of these events I maintained my position as an ambassador of the team, meeting and greeting fans worldwide who made the trek to "Mecca" which I called Oakland for the games. Even language barriers didn't keep me from sharing the love and attempting to enhance their game day experiences, taking photos which became their proof of meeting me and sharing their stories with family and friends from the many places they had traveled from around the world. I felt honored to be a part of their memories to be shared all over the world. To my surprise, the tailgating rituals were much the same as I'd been a part of in Los Angeles with it being family oriented gatherings where everyone shared what they brought, how the lines would form overnight waiting for the gates to open the following morning and the numerous parties that jumped off up and down these lines of vehicles. There was always some fellowshipping going on around the stadium, even if you were from out of town you'd be welcomed like family to join in the festivities which till this day I'm proud of because generally we get such a bad reputation for being thugs and deviants when we're just misunderstood for the way of life that we live and the manners in which we express our loyalty to the team. My constant suggestion to those opposing fans is to break bread with us and really get to know us before coming to conclusions based on stories you've heard usually from people looking from the outside who mostly form their opinions on hearsay rather than personal experience. I feel that after fellowshipping with us, you'll have a different opinion of us because we're just as family friendly as the next fan base, thus my mission continues to educate the masses an ambassador. During a commercial shoot for Coca-Cola I remember the director explaining to me how his father who was a famous Hollywood director himself had told him growing up that if you could do something that you truly enjoyed and got paid for it that it wouldn't feel like work so the idea came to my mind of possibly becoming the team's official mascot. After speaking with an employee who said that I'd have to possibly wear something that completely covered my body so you couldn't tell my gender or ethnicity that idea didn't seem as illustrious as before I heard these words, but I continued doing things my way with the character I had developed with idea that as one door closes another opens and to always be prepared when it does. A friend and former football player who worked for one of the major television networks advised me to keep doing my thing just the way I had been because it would allow me the freedoms that I wouldn't have if I were employed with the team, meaning there would be many stipulations which would take the fun out of what I was doing and assured me it was working and to just stick with it. Thank you for that advice my friend, you know who you are and I appreciated the conversation. While working on a project at Direct TV in El Segundo, California I ran into one of the main executives for the company who was explaining to the guys on my crew how we would be paying to watch sports on television in the near future, which we laughed about and said he was crazy. He assured us that this would be the wave of the future and called it pay-per-view, but through meeting this executive got a part in their commercial that they shot in the same building we were working on. When the NFL Network was launched, I got another opportunity to be in one of their first commercials where I shared a scene with the famous musician Tim McGraw. He was a terrific guy who asked me if my face paint was hypoallergenic, I told him that I wasn't sure but it stayed on until I took it off which he had a good laugh about. We had a blast shooting the commercial where I recited the Autumn Wind representing the Raiders. I kept my eyes focused looking for opportunities where I could further establish my character throughout the industry. With my adventures at work remaining a constant, I moved between companies doing my best

Day of Worship

to keep a low profile, do my work so I could hope-fully stretch out my time before being let go to beat the bush for another job opportunity and continued to find a way to make my trips to Oakland for the games. Around 1993 I started a screen-printing busi-ness out of my garage to both bring in some extra cash and to further along my passion for my clothing designs, after attending an expo within the garment industry. I didn't have the necessary funding for my start up equipment so I borrowed enough to pur-chase my first printing machine and a belt dryer for curing the ink used on my designs and a few screens used in the printing process to get started. I began to search for local jobs between the schools and businesses in my area, and began designing fan gear for the youth football teams around town because most parents wanted custom designs and not that cor-porate apparel sold by the youth organization. It took a while before I was print-ing jobs and building my resume in the area of Rancho Cucamonga, California and gaining their confidence in the quality of my work and the fair prices at which I did them. What this turn of events did was fuel my desire to start my own clothing line, an idea I'd had since my high school days when I was drawing and or painting custom designs on my schoolmates' clothes from school making a little extra pocket money. Also when I was competing on the bodybuilding circuit I wanted to have my own custom designs dedicated to the sport, not wanting to wear the same designs that were being sold at that time so I began to draw from a creature I fell in love with as a kid watching the cartoon Johnny Quest. That creature was a Komodo dragon, which in the cartoon was walked on a huge leash made of chains by one of the main characters. Mesmerized by the size and strength of these dragons, I took it as my company mascot and till this day it still represents the methodical tenacity I apply to my daily life. I dreamed of owning a Komodo dragon until this guy at a reptile store informed me that it was an endangered species, a deadly predator and I could go to prison if caught with one. After doing my research am convinced that this was true, but still admire the tenacity and focus of these beautiful creatures. Even though ending my competitive body-building career in 1989 I still loved to throw the weights around and wearing sports gear of my own design was very gratifying to me as it was just another piece of the puzzle connected on the journey. My dream is to have my clothing worn by athletes and fitness enthusiasts around the world. My work load with the printing grew to the point where I would get home from work, grab a quick bite and go right into my garage where I would print orders sometimes until midnight getting up around 3 a.m. to prepare for my regular job in construction. This continued for a few years until I was diagnosed with walking pneumonia by my doctor and was advised to cut back on my activities or he'd be forced

Entrance to "Cellblock" D

to admit me into the hospital for about a week to get rest and recovery. I made him a promise to scale back on the hours I was putting in after work, which wasn't the easiest thing to do when you've got t-shirt orders pilling up with deadlines looming, so I did my best to complete each order and deliver them to my customers in a timely manner. In May of 1998 my mom and brother flew out to California for my daughter's graduation from high school and got a close look at my printing operation and were amazed at how everything took place from drawing people's designs, developing the necessary screens needed for each job, purchasing the garments and inks from the suppliers, then printing the jobs. I'd promised my mom that I would continue using my gift for an Art and my brother reminded me of the talks we'd had about owning our own enterprise someday, saying this could be that business. A short time following their visit things at home began to deteriorate rapidly to the point that upon advisement from a law enforcement officer who I'd called to my house to investigate some missing items, which was my costume that I wore to the games moved out and shut down my screen printing business until I saw where things were heading and after a lengthy period of court proceedings got divorced and went through a long process of starting over with my life. Believe me when I tell you, every story you've ever heard about divorce is just someone else's story until it becomes your story where you are one of the performers but not in full control of the script. I wouldn't wish an episode like this on my worst enemy. I tried to shelter my kids from the meltdown, but I'm sure that they knew things weren't the same around the house. I buried myself in my printing jobs or lifting weights as a form of therapy just to keep my mind, body and spirit in unison. Even my mom said when they were there for the graduation you could've cut the tension with a knife because there wasn't any laughter and very little conversation between us, usually when we got together it was like a comic review. I was in shock just looking into places to rent and purchasing furniture and the like because I hadn't dealt with renting since 1982, so the whole idea of searching for new living quarters while continuing to work as much as possible, and having to go through purchasing furniture and appliances put my head in a very dark place especially when I'd left a house full of furniture behind. Even my co-workers noticed a change in my attitude during this period of time and would ask why I seemed on edge all of a sudden, but never explaining my marital situation to them. My never give up attitude wouldn't let me fail, so little by little I slowly got back on my feet with a thirst to get back into my own home someday, which my mom always assured me that there was another house with my name on it but I had to crawl for a while before standing up to walk again. She told me there would be a different level of appreciation when I could stand up and walk again. Hard words to hear but deep inside I knew she had the wisdom far greater than my own plus the experience firsthand so I took her advice to heart and began to set my sites on the future and my next house. During this time, I ended up landing a job with the construction division of the City of Los Angeles through my union while the City Hall building was being remodeled in 2000 where they needed experienced tradesmen to complete this project. My union rep told me I was perfect for the job because of my years in the ceiling trade, so my hours were long averaging 72 per week but I didn't mind because it took my mind off the separation and pending divorce proceedings. So stock piling as much of my earnings as possible with the incredible amount of overtime on the City Hall project, I rededicated myself to getting back to the point where I could consider house hunting again. This process took about seven years as I had to clear up my credit and satisfy a debt to the Internal Revenue Service. Working for the city gave me a whole new perspective of all the moving parts and the politics involved in city management, as we had some very strict rules as far as how the remodeling project was conducted. Rules that the average citizens didn't have privy to and that I'd never dealt with since beginning my career in the construction industry in August of 1978. There were a lot of moving parts who behind the scenes coordinated this project from start to finish to whom it benefitted the workers not to know, because in coming into contact with said persons meant that you'd cross the line of someone of high ranking and would be disciplined sometimes to the extent of termination of your employment. Also getting caught leaving the jobsite before the evening bell was sounded was immediate termination, or taking any items from the dumpster even if you may have considered it to be trash. My biggest dilemma while on the project was the pace at which I was getting my work done. Now you'd think maybe my work pace was too slow, but it was just the opposite as several other contractors on the project and even my foreman had said on several occasions to just slow down and follow the pace of everyone else on the job which took a while for me to grasp because through my years of experience in the industry you were never fast enough. So in trying to show my efficiency and expertise often got me sent before supervision who informed me that by completing my work too fast wasn't setting well with some of the other contractors on the project who carried a lot of weight, and continuing to cross them would get me demoted or worst yet taken off the project all together. On one particular occasion I was sent to the top of the City Hall building just to keep me on the jobsite, but out of sight of the contractors who weren't very happy with me at that time. For a week I reported to work, signed in, grabbed my tools even though they weren't being used and go directly to the roof until coffee break, lunch and the afternoon break before signing out at the end of the shift. As my curiosity for the Catalina Islands which I could see from the top of City Hall grew, took a trip with Bertha to spend the weekend and remember her getting sea sick on the way over, but after arriving she began to feel better and we enjoyed the stay there. Even if you had a legitimate reason for leaving work early, they frowned on it because it messed up their headcount for that day. Long

Wife and I on GameDay

story made short, that City Hall project was one of my most memorable jobs during my 36+ years in construction and the lessons I'll never forget as to how the "city" construction operations function. As my time with that project came to an end I was assigned to a few other city projects installing or repairing ceilings until eventually being let go and once again searching for another landing spot for work, not wanting to break the momentum gained during my time with the City of Los Angeles so I was making daily phone calls to my union stewards to find employment opportunities for me. Meanwhile we took a vacation to Hawaii for quick, fun-filled week that was like a trip to paradise. It was all the beauty of California on steroids, lush tropical plants, beautiful beaches and caves, fabulous luaus where the feast of foods was endless. Plus, the hospitality was outstanding as several business owners reminded us that most of their earnings depended on tourism, something they didn't take for granted. You actually forgot about time while there just soaking in every moment and adventure we encountered, which began each morning grabbing a quick bite before heading to the beautiful Waikiki beaches. We would enjoy cocktails at the beachside bars while the kids enjoyed boogie boarding and building sand castles for most of the morning. Next it was off to one of several excursions we had signed up to attend during our stay on the island. The first excursion took us to a remote part of the interior where numerous movies had been filmed, the lush forest and tropical settings were breath taking with awesome waterfalls that could remember from some of the movies our tour guide told our group about. Next morning repeated itself before we took another excursion to the North shore of the island where we enjoyed riding horses along this trail at the edge of a cliff overlooking the beaches occupied by the surfers who were catching some fantastic waves crashing the shores. The horse our guide picked for me to ride was the largest one in the stable, plus he wore a metal basket around his mouth because he would bite and when I asked why they picked this particular horse for me, the guide told me because of my weight we were a perfect match. Everyone got a big laugh out of it except me who was wondering how this horse and I were going to get alone. So off we go on this trail and we were amazed at how the horses navigated this narrow trail, even as they stumbled on a few loose rocks. Being that this was my very first ride on a horse and especially one this large, my adrenaline was sky high until one of the guides told me to show the horse that I was in control by squeezing him with my legs. As soon as I tried what she said he looks around at me and she told me that he had gotten the message, amazing how smart these animals are. Bertha's horse decides that it's ready to go back to the stable about halfway through the ride and turns around in a full gallop causing her to scream for help, so one of the guides had to catch up to the horse and make it get back in line to finish the tour. Completing our adventure with the horses, went back into town for dinner and walking along the beach watching the magnificent sunsets. Even at night the island was bustling with people enjoying the cool tropical breezes as they partied at clubs and luaus. A day of snorkeling was next and spending time on some of the most beautiful reefs we had ever seen, the water so clear you could see huge fish and other sea life swimming right around us as we stood waist deep in the ocean. Our day ended with us taking a sunset catamaran a few miles out into the ocean, which also had a group of corporate workers onboard who didn't really take advantage of the moments. After making friends with the captain and crew, we got the party started along with a couple Frank and Maureen that we met onboard who just happen to be Raiders fans. As the waves got bigger as we rode out to destination to watch the magnificent sunset, I decided to jump out into this huge net attached to the front of the boat and persuaded the kids to join me for an exhilarating wet ride. We enjoyed the experience hanging on to the net as the frigid waves crashed into us while the captain had the music blasting over the sound system. I remember the captain thanking us for making the excursion a fun one for them upon returning to shore because that corporate group was boring to him and wondered why they even took the cruise because all they did was sit and watch our group having a good time. Meantime we continued partying with the couple we met back at their hotel which was right on Waikiki beach, with a balcony that surrounded their hotel suite. They were island hopping so we never saw them again but still keep in touch today and as our week came to an end, we had to pack for the flight back home. During this time, I had the pleasure of working with FOX SPORTS on several occasions appearing in segments of their Sunday morning show. The coolest part of the experience was when they would send a limousine to my home to pick me up in full game day attire and bring me to the studios, and always got compensation for missing work which I respected from them. My employers understood that I was making history and never gave me grief when any of the media outlets would call me for my services. The limo drivers would get a kick when they pulled up to the security gates and roll down the window to show them who was sitting in back. On set in the studios I never knew just what they would have me doing but always rose to the occasion and on one of my visits ran into one of my colleagues from Jackson State who was working for the network after finishing his football career with the Rams. He got a big laugh when I told him who I was because he had been seeing me on television for years. My persistence in looking for work paid off with me getting hired by one of the biggest and best-known ceiling contractors in Southern California, who had made a name for themselves by the notable projects and the high quality of work they'd been doing for quite a few years. I felt honored to have gotten an opportunity to establish myself as a committed, dependable employee with this company but was put to the test right from the beginning as I had to prove myself all over again doing what we called in the industry apprentice work. Though it didn't set well with me at all because I felt that my years of experience warranted me running projects, had to tighten my chin strap, buckle down and remember that I'd dealt with this in the past and there was no one to go crying to because the usual response from the union was just be glad that you're working. Here again being an outsider with no connections in the industry I had to hold my own, having only my work to speak for me as far as my fortitude and character were concerned. We had projects at some of the best universities, hospitals, movie studios, airports and amusement parks all over southern California and had the opportunity to work there a little more than eight years and made a good living before being let go. My last chapter of my construction career had me bouncing from company to company again while dealing with the physical pain I had been suffering with for over six years, until being hired by a general contractor out of Las Vegas, Nevada to work on a project at a Marine base out in the California desert town of 29 Palms which was around eighty six miles one way for me to drive each day. After meeting a few guys from the other trades, I started carpooling with one of the drywall installers who lived in Perris, California named Sam. We definitely had some good trips to and from the desert, once getting pulled over by a CHP officer who after checking out my license discovered that he and his kids had taken photos with me at the Raiders vs Chargers game in San Diego. All the while the officer and I were talking my carpool buddy Sam's facial expression was asking what the hell this officer was talking about at the game. I hadn't told Sam that I was the Violator at the Raiders games, so when the officer gave us an escort to our exit to 29 Palms and flashed his lights saying goodbye, just looked me and said you never know who you're talking to. Before that day was over, I think everyone on the project had heard of his discovery. The beautiful thing about that was meeting not only Raiders fans but fans of just about all thirty-two NFL teams, which ended up being some great conversations over the course of the job. It was difficult for them to get and keep local workers from the unions in Los Angeles because of the driving distance and the brutal desert heat in the summer. Even Eric, the guy that ran our crew installing the ceilings eventually left the project and I was selected to finish running the crew until I was the only ceiling installer left on the project. I almost became a victim of the heat when I was overcome by heat exhaustion and had to be packed with ice packs to prevent me from passing out. I'm talking outside temperatures in the upper 80s to low 90s at the start of our workday and up in the ceilings where I worked got over 110 degrees with no air conditioning. This wasn't anything new because it had happened before on a project in Indio, California during the summer where I endured extreme dehydration and muscle spasms working in buildings with no air conditioning. My medical provider informed me that the sports drinks I had been consuming while at work weren't helping with my hydration, rather adding to the problem. During this time, I got the results of an MRI that I had taken earlier and upon viewing them with an orthopedic specialist, who advised me to retire because of the irreversible damage to my disc, coincided with my being released from the project because of funding issues between the government and the contractor. Talk about one door closing and another one opening, I drew down my disability for a year before filing for retirement in 2013. Getting my total disability awarded was another ordeal because on my first court date I was profiled by the judge and his comments taken down by the stenographer in the minutes came back to bite him in the end. The law firm who represented me out of Boston, Massachusetts is another one of my guardian angels as they ramped up the pressure on this judge after he pushed my case back just because he felt like I should still be working, even after advisement from the vocational specialist from my union brought in for their expert opinion of my work status. The vocation specialist showed him on a graft my work history and with the heavy labor demand plus the years put in the trade that I was done working, which caused her to receive a death stare from the judge. Months went by before I could get another day in court to hopefully get my total disability granted and by now the lead attorney for the firm sent out an attorney who they called a closer and assured me that the outcome would be different today. They told me that the medical evidence was sufficient enough to award me and after listening to the remarks the judge made, knew that I had been racially profiled and intended to make an example out of him for his statement and delaying my case for over a year. I remember meeting my new attorney and he said don't worry because today you're going to get paid so just sit back and relax because we got him by the balls. As the court begins, the judge had a different vocational specialist in hoping to hear a different analogy than the one before meanwhile I had signed a form agreeing to pay every attorney in the firm a percentage of my award which would come from the state. We go through the whole proceeding and upon hearing the same analysis from the second specialist stared her down like he did the one before, my attorney looked over at me and smiled. When the judge got to the last sheet, which was the one I signed that morning, you could see a lump in his throat as he asked the attorney does this mean I have to pay twenty-two attorneys this amount? He glances at me as if to say, you signed off on this as he could hardly get the words out to tell me that my total disability had been granted. I called this day my 'Deliverance' because now I didn't have to stress about my finances anymore. Now even though my work history had its peaks and valleys, my only constant was making the trips to Oakland for my weekly "Therapy" during the football seasons which had gained me some notoriety through the media coverage, television commercials, guest appearances, etc. Even the owner of the company that I had worked for previously made a comment on my commitment, and the passion I'd shown for my team and that it never seemed to interfere with my performance on the job, which was kind of a jab at the guys who had plenty of excuses as to why they couldn't make it to work, especially on Mondays. He knew of me making my trips to Oakland for the football games and still being at work on time regardless of the time I returned. I guess I'd earned his respect in regards to how serious I took both my work and leisure and how I was dedicated to both. This became more apparent as stories of my traveling back and forth to Raiders games began to come out through the media outlets, as I was doing sit down interviews with notable organizations like ESPN, FOX, CBS, HBO and others to get a more intimate look into what I was all about. It was interesting to me how I would be contacted for my opinions on matters pertaining to the team, and I would always try to give my answers based on the fans' point of view, but with the understanding that we're talking about big business and that I wasn't sure of how much weight the fans opinions even carried but always answered honestly as to how we the fans looked at each matter. I think that relationship with the media world has grown as time has passed and I only wanted to be remembered as an ambassador for the team. The year of 2000 my "Fandom" rose to a new level when I was inducted into the Visa Hall of Fans at the Pro Football Hall of Fame in Canton, Ohio after writing an essay on how I looked at the game and how I saw my character as a part of the fabric of the game. You couldn't even imagine my excitement when the letter came letting me know of Visa's decision to induct me into the Hall of Fame as the Raiders fan representative, right then I felt like I truly had earned the title of ambassador and just as exciting was traveling to Canton in full gear on the plane with just my "war-paint" kit and toiletries for the three day trip of a lifetime. As a thank you to my friend Tim who had paid for some of my flights to the games in Oakland, took him with me to Canton as my guest. Meeting the fans selected from the other thirty-one teams around the league was beyond awesome as many of us had only seen each other through television, but now being able to get to know one another felt like this fraternity of ambassadors like no other and as we were taken through our weekend schedule of events leading up to the actual induction ceremony I think we all will share the memories of that weekend together forever. I remember speaking to my local sports media live back in Los Angeles during the induction ceremony and being thankful for the opportunity of being selected as one of the best at what I did, which was just being a "DIE-HARD" fan and ambassador for my team. I looked at my chance to make a difference in the way fans enjoyed their game day experiences, but also looked at the opportunity to plant some seeds along the way and hopefully live long enough to witness the harvest in the future.

Chapter 5

These life experiences had begun to help me formulate a plan moving forward in my journey that I constantly try to share with the people whose paths I'm blessed to cross in hopes of leaving some positive footprints, a promise I made to myself while attending my father's funeral in November of 1995 back in Arkansas. We had just driven back to Mound Bayou the previous summer for a family reunion and noticed how thin my dad was, but he seemed happy just seeing all of us and our kids at our reunion so I didn't give it much thought plus he'd never been one to complain about pain being that tough army guy he was. I found out later that he had small cell lung cancer, thought to be from his exposure to Agent Orange while in the military. But after two surgeries, the first where they removed one of his lungs and he never healed properly and while conducting the second one discovered the cancer had spread to his other lung the doctors suggested to him to do whatever he wanted because there was nothing else they could do at that point. A few months later he lost his battle and passed away and my brother let me know to get home for his burial. As we're sitting in the front pew as the funeral proceedings commenced I just remembered the emotions running through me as my thoughts went back to our journey together even through the rough times of how he was driven by a force never spoken of, and had his own unique way of trying to teach my brother and I about life and some of its lessons to be learned but I looked at it as his fear of failure and attempting to bridge the gap between us created by the divorce. Ending his life's journey at the young age of sixty-two kind of hit home with me in a way that further ignited the fire already burning inside of me to do something with my life and to leave behind some footprints worthy of following when it was all said and done for my time in this world. What really bothered me the most was that out of a full church only two people got up to say how he had affected their lives just by knowing him. We

69

had to take his casket and put it in the bed of a pickup truck to get it up the hill to his gravesite and even standing graveside there was tension in the air as I threw my fist full of dirt over his casket on this cold and windy day and said goodbye. Returning to his mom's house for the family gathering this fire that was suddenly turned all the way up wouldn't allow me to enjoy the conversations, so I told one of our cousins to take us for a ride to try and cool off to no avail. Upon returning home I told my first wife that either you're with me or against me because from that moment going forward, I became totally focused on accomplishing as many of my goals as possible before the sand in my hour glass runs out. It seemed as if my words had fallen on deft ears, so the struggles continued on for years until the day the sheriff I called to investigate a possible theft of my costume that I wore to the games took me outside to inquire about any marital issues. He went on to explain the path that we were headed on and advised me to find someplace else to live before things escalated into a domestic violence call, and after being booked on those charges I would be treated different by law enforcement whenever my license was ran. He also suggested for me to make a phone call to her relatives to leave a message that I had called the sheriff department over about my missing costume. Well I made the call and the next evening when I returned home from work there was my costume thrown across the garage floor but it had been mysteriously returned just in time for a trip to Oakland for a game. Now you talk about sleeping with one eye open, that's exactly how I slept until being able to find an apartment to rent on the other side of town which took about a week, securing the keys and moving out taking only my clothes and a small television. I packed everything into my Silverado pickup to drive away, but my son got home from school before I could leave and asked me what was going on. I explained to him that I had to move out until the situation between his mom and I could be worked out, but he came to visit once I got settled into my new apartment. I think that was really a plot to find out where I'd moved to because soon after had to get a restraining order placed on my estranged wife. And as I turned the page one this chapter of my life another quickly began as I was introduced to a young lady who would eventually become my second wife, after a lengthy courtship. One lesson learned from past experiences taught me that when two people pull their cart in opposite directions a split form and eventually the cart falls apart, sort of like when a dog chases its tail, running in a circle going nowhere and never catching that tail. So as I was in the process of regaining some order to my life she was always there lending both advice and support when needed, which was like a breath of fresh air because even with trying to move on after my divorce I was skeptical about getting involved with anyone in a serious relationship. And even as I continued to deal with issues working and re-establishing my credit so I could pursue buying another house, she always supported my decisions along the way. The best thing about her was that we became best friends long before we ever took the relationship further, doing all types of activities together with her kids which wasn't anything new for me because of the years with my own kids and their activities at school their participation in sports during the time I was there. I always managed to get them to and from their activities even if there were printing jobs to be finished and made sure that they ate before going to bed. So the whole idea helping with her kids never bothered me because I'd walked these roads before and any lessons I could share with them just felt normal as a parent. On our first actual date I'd asked her to attend a football game with me to which she agreed so I intentionally didn't explain to her how I dressed for the games as the "Violator" to see what kind of reaction I would get from her. I was actually more nervous about the reaction from her than the normal butterflies you get on a game day, so as I pulled up to her house around 6:00 a.m. on a foggy Sunday morning and rang the doorbell I'm saying to myself "Violator" hear goes whatever my man. The look from her I fully expected, as I'm standing at her door in full war-paint and game day gear telling her it's time for our road trip to San Diego. She looked me over a couple of times with her jaw dropped as did her kids before we got in my low-rider Silverado and headed south for the Raiders vs Chargers football game. I noticed how close she sat toward the passenger side door gripping the handle as we're cruising down the 15 freeway, after a while I had to break the ice by letting her know that I wouldn't bite her if she relaxed a bit, the whole time she's observing a sort of caravan forming on the freeway all with Raiders flags, decals, banners, music blaring and blowing their horns and waiving at us. I knew she was beginning to wonder where the hell I was taking her when she asked me if I knew all those people honking at us, so I told her that they were part of the family and we'd meet some of the others when we arrived at the stadium. Now mind you, the expression on her face was saying what kind of family is this? As we got closer to the stadium our caravan grew tremendously to the point where we were backed up on the freeway off ramp for what seemed like a mile just waiting to enter the stadium parking lot, so people were getting out of their vehicles walking up and down the line shaking hands and exchanging pleasantries as we always do when we're in a waiting situation, it's the excitement of the tailgating experience and to miss that is cutting yourself short of the whole game day rituals for us as fans. You could hear the music bumping from the parking lots even before we got off the freeway so I knew that we were there in full force on this day and tried to hold back my excitement until we could get to our final destination in lot N3 which we called the village because it had become the most popular areas around the stadium, but actually you could find Raiders fans all around the parking lot where it looked like a home game for us. Even as we're cruising along trying to get parked people are coming up to my truck greeting us and I'm watching her reaction to all of this because once I parked it would really get crazy. Once we got to our parking spot and we got out of my truck it was like a welcoming committee headed toward us, people bringing all types of pre-game libations and the likes over to us as I introduced her to the kindred spirits I called family. They welcomed her with open arms as we began to get our tailgating revved up before taking that passion inside the stadium. As I began taking photos with everyone even the opposing fans, eating some delicious food and just enjoying the fellowship the time seemed to fly by and before you knew it, we had to head inside for the game. Now as we approach the gates to enter the stadium things got pretty intense because somehow I ended up against a wall spread eagle by the stadium security as they patted me down to the dismay of the other fans standing there watching the whole fiasco, even to the point where they made me take off part of my costume and leave it in their security office until the game was over claiming that I might hurt someone. There was one officer standing on top of the entrance with an assault rifle advising our fans to pipe down while they continued to make an example of me because of how I was dressed. This situation had stemmed from a photo and article written by a reporter basically implying that I was the leader of this hoard of Raiders fans, so the security in San Diego was on the lookout for me to make an example to the rest of our fans because they really hated how we dressed in all type of costumes to show our passion and it really pissed off their fans. My then girlfriend was looking at me like do you go through this at every stadium and my reply to her was no just here which as upset as I was, wasn't going to give them the power to rain on my parade. So, as we get to finally go through the gates, I told them to enjoy themselves and I'd see them after the game for the rest of my gear, so after our team winning that game just made the whole event more enjoyable to me. By now I'm still trying to feel my girlfriend Bertha's perception of our date thus far which was hard to put my finger on, but as we began our journey back to Rancho Cucamonga, she finally admitted that even with the drama at the entry gates she had really enjoyed herself. I reminded her that it would only get better as we continued along this journey together espe-cially traveling to Oakland for the games and still to this day, I'm trying to hold true to that promise of "Enjoying the Moments!" Making it back to town and dropping her off at home we ended our day on a high note, and couldn't wait for the next adventure which came with the next game this time in Oakland. That next trip to Oakland was fantastic as we celebrated all the events around Raider Mecca, a celebration before the season home opener. The celebration closes with a huge party at Ricky's sports bar in San Leandro where the crowd was so big it poured out into the parking lot. We danced the night away before returning to our hotel to prepare for the opening game on Sunday. Slowly my journey starts to swing in an upward direction, giving me the determination to make this time we spent together as special as the first every time and can say I've truly been blessed. Our next adventure begins when we're heading back to Canton, Ohio for the Hall of Fame reunion 2001. After carefully packing my gear in a special container for our trip, not wanting to deal with wearing it the whole time like before and we get to the O'Hare International airport in Chicago, we were informed that no more flights would be leaving until the next morning and here's when the adventure gets turned up a notch or two. We had to be in Canton early the next day for a parade for the new inductees into the Hall of Fame, so with no connecting flights our only option was to rent a vehicle at one way rates to drive all night to be able to arrive in town, check-in my hotel, get dressed in my gear and get to the parade spot. After renting a car I had to collect our luggage to make this drive through the turnpike system into Canton, the airport workers can't seem to find my luggage and already being in mission-a- go mode tried my best not get arrested as I took offense to the airline not being able to find the luggage we'd just dropped off with them not more than an hour before. But even with my restraint still was giving the attendant a hard time suggesting that I may have needed to go back there accompanied by the supervisor to help them find my gear. Funny how people's journeys cross paths because during the ordeal with finding my gear we ran into this lady named Joy who was on her way to Canton for the same ceremony, and after meeting us asked if she could ride along with us. We welcomed her as if we'd known her for years to come along with us on this adventure which didn't bother her at all. Everyone's luggage finally being located and packed in the car, we begin driving through what seemed like a hundred turnpikes and not long after we stopped to grab a bite to eat in Indiana fast food restaurant. As we stood in line waiting to place our order, Joy noticed that we never got called to put our food order in and she told one of the clerks that we were with her and that we'd like to place an order if they didn't mind. Right away I knew we had picked up our guardian angel to make sure we made it to our destination safely, and that inci-dent really broke the ice and let us converse on some deep subject matter all the way to Canton. Upon reaching our hotel which was a few miles away from our passenger's hotel there was a message on the phone in my room instructing me what time I needed to be in position for the parade, which barely left me time to change into my game day attire and drive to our parade location. To this day that's the fastest I've ever transformed into my character the "Violator", but we made it to the parade site just in time for me to jump on the float they had for us to ride on while Bertha had to sort of walk through the immense crowd that turned out to watch the parade as she followed the float that we characters rode on. I remember trying to keep an eye on her throughout the whole parade as she would disappear winding her way around some of the heavier sections of people, thinking to myself how this woman took on each adventure as just coming with the territory and telling myself she was a keeper. The route was pretty long and lasted quite a while and by the time it ended we had built up a big appetite which got nourished at the dinner party they threw for us later in the afternoon where everyone got to meet and greet as we enjoyed the cuisine prepared for our group. But before any of this took place there was the Hall of Fame induction ceremony to attend where all the excitement came to a boiling point as each inductee got introduced, got up and made their speeches while the fans gave them gracious applause and cheers for being recognized as the best at what they'd done during their professional careers. After the conclusion of the induction ceremony and meeting some of the inductees, taking photos and just soaking in what we had witnessed and been a part of got to get changed and cleaned up for the awesome dinner prepared for us where everyone got to break bread and truly fellowship with one another. Some remained in town for the Hall of Fame game the next day but we drove to the airport for our flight back to California. Just as we thought our adventures had ended, while waiting on our return flight my girlfriend got called up to the boarding gate by airport security as I was instructed to stay in my seat. As the security officers spoke with her, the expression on her face was of sheer panic and surprise prompting me to walk over to find out what was going on. They had been inquiring if we had been in contact with any contraband while in Canton, stating that they had found traces of contraband on my luggage. I stated the nature of our visit to Canton and assured them that this discovery had absolutely nothing to do with either of us and I didn't appreciate how they had scared the hell out of my girlfriend, thinking she would snitch on me out of fear from the questioning. We were allowed to board our flight after an apology for the misunderstanding, but Bertha was convinced that traveling with me anywhere was an adventure of its own and she concluded that I just had the look of a bad guy. Overall that reunion trip to Canton was one for the books in our minds, but through the whole thing we met a beautiful lady named Joy who just happen to be the CPA for a famous NFL player in the Bay area, and as a thank you for letting her ride with us to Canton from Chicago sent us a pair of complimentary tickets to a football game in San Francisco when the Raiders played them there. Upon making the trip to the stadium in San Francisco for the game and enjoying a fantastic tailgate with other Raiders fans, we head towards the gates to enter the stadium and here comes the drama with security, putting me through the paces about my costume, bending my spikes, checking out my boots saying they could be used to harm someone. As you can imagine where Bertha's mind has gone by now as she has witness such scrutiny of my costume before trying to enter football games, but one of the supervisors said to let me in because it was causing a big commotion at the gates as the Raiders fans got enraged by their actions. Once inside the stadium and we're soaking up the ambience of the place walking to our complimentary seats, some of the home team fans began to question us about how we'd gotten tickets in their area. I explained to them that the tickets were from someone connected with a player from their team, which didn't go over well with the fans and wouldn't you know before we could take our seats four police officers walked up to us and said we were to remain seated for the entire game and if we stood up we would be escorted out of the stadium. You can imagine the applause they got from the fans, which looked a lot like discrimination but I knew it was because of the team I represented. I'm thinking to myself here's another mark on my record with my girl not counting what took place at the entry gate but this incident had upset her to the point that she had some choice words for the police as they flanked us on both isles daring us to stand up and the lady sitting in front of us who was so drunk and spitting in my face never heard a word from the police. For this reason, I don't care to ever visit that stadium again. A big thank you to Joy who sent us the tickets certainly not thinking our reception would be anything of this nature but it made clear what I'd been told before about the ongoing feud in the Bay area. This was my worst experience in an NFL stadium to date and us winning the game on a last second field goal was poetic justice as the same group of fans who had antagonized us the entire game were nowhere to be found when the ball went through the goal posts. Even the officers who had given us a stern warning were gone as we turn to exit the stadium, so making it back to our car headed back to Rancho Cucamonga to prepare for work the following day. In spite of the adventures previously spoken of I was in a good place in life, work was plentiful, my relationship was cruising along at a great pace and my team was having a great season making it to the playoffs. Adventure wasn't done with us yet as I got a phone call on the morning of our home playoff game against the Titans which I didn't have tickets for, was instructed to get a flight to Oakland because there were two tickets waiting for me at the will call window. Mind you we're still in bed and wondering if we could even book a flight so close to game time, and after calling every airport in the area was able to get the only flight getting us to Oakland in time for the game out of John Wayne airport in Irvine, California which is when my old friend adventure stopped by for a visit. Transforming into my character the "Violator" as quickly as possible and driving to the airport, I was greeted by security and asked to step out of line and follow them, leaving Bertha wondering what the hell was happening. We had noticed how the whole terminal took pause as I walked in and got in line to board the plane, joking about it as we usually did but on this occasion some of the other passengers had stated that they weren't going to board the same flight as the guy dressed in the spiked shoulder pads and face paint. So as the security took me towards an elevator to go through a more personal security check in a private room, I asked a worker for the airline what the commotion was all about especially with an officer carrying an assault rifle standing guard at the door as they put me through the paces. He laughed as he told me the controversy was over me getting on the plane dressed in war-gear and after a thorough inspection instructed me to board the plane and stand behind the partition in the back of the plane where the attendants served refreshments until everyone else had boarded the plane, then quietly get in the seats they had set aside for us on the plane. Remember this was shortly after the 9-11 fiasco so everyone was dealing with the memories of the attack and were on edge especially in my case where I'd never flown out of this airport in my costume, so I guess it caused the panic at the terminal but as we made the flight to Oakland my rewards for being such a good sport through the whole ordeal was complimentary beverages for the entire flight. Arriving in Oakland we were pushed for time to get to the stadium and pick up the playoff tickets at will call, get through security and try to make it to our seats before the game started so we took the BART over to the stadium, got to will call as quickly as possible and just made it to our seats as the Nation Anthem was performed. The atmosphere in the Coliseum was crazy loud as it had been a few years since we had been in the playoffs so the joint was rocking! The AFC Divisional game against the Titans was one of those down to the wire victories for us, and the intensity was to the point I got a face full of Gatorade from one of the Titans players after the game and when I asked the security hadn't they seen the incident, both of them said he's going home and your team's going to the Super Bowl. Returning home, we couldn't believe the events leading up to this day, and I started saying "You can't make this stuff up" when we experience other moments like the ones we had been going through together. So here the Raiders are in the Super Bowl against the Buccaneers in San Diego, California and the big question I was hearing constantly was would I be attending the game, from family, friends and the media alike. My constant answer was that I couldn't afford tickets to the game, but it would be nice to somehow gain entrance into the game. During the week leading up to the game I'd been driving down to San Diego doing interviews with local sports shows and even doing a special piece with NFL Films where I had to walk on the field which didn't set well with the security or the grounds keepers there because of our team's history. The film crew couldn't believe the response they got when they presented our passes to get on the field to film the piece which was being broadcast live over in Tokyo, Japan, so eventually we were escorted down on the playing field and allowed to film. After completing the mission the crew invited me to join them for dinner to polish of a successful day, where the question of me getting tickets to the Super Bowl and again I told them that the only way I could attend the game was if I had tickets donated because I couldn't afford them. They took me to a well know sports bar in San Diego and were blown away that the treatment there was similar to what they experienced just hours ago at the stadium shoot. We filmed another skit at the airport in San Diego where it appeared to be a kidnapping which was hilarious because the actual travelers weren't sure if it was real or not, to the director's delight. I got to do some more work with that film crew on another occasion that week where I accompanied them to an event at the Convention center where again there were questions about me and my friend 'Toozak' gaining entry into the event even though they presented a pass for us to be with the crew for this event. After making a phone call to police headquarters by the Lead person of the film crew we were allowed to enter the exclusive event where we were greeted by the Hall of Fame wide receiver Jerry Rice who welcomed us with open arms and invited us into his event. I just remember the expression on the officer's face who told me and my good friend 'Toozak' to stand over to the side when his boss told him on the phone to allow us to enter the event with the film crew, if looks could kill. Upon driving back to San Diego for another event on Friday before the big game I was approached by a sportscaster from ABC sports and asked whether or not I had tickets for the game, and after telling him no decided to do a segment about me this "DIE-HARD" fan for the Raiders not being able to attend the Super Bowl, stating how many complimentary tickets each team had at their disposal and just felt like I deserved to get into the game. Having nothing to lose I agreed to do the segment live on their evening sports coverage. I thought it was tastefully done and was thankful for his generosity in giving me such a platform in hopes of tickets being sent my way, but to no avail so my girlfriend and I watched the game with our friends the Smiths at their house. On another trip down to San Diego during the week leading up to the big game I appeared as a guest on The Best Damn Sports Show where again the question was brought up about me attending the game which I honestly couldn't answer at that time. Missing out on watching that Super Bowl game in person still bothers me till this day being that it was in my backyard, plus my team was playing in it so I made a promise to myself that the next time my team made it to the big dance I would find a way to attend if I was still alive. We maintained our season tickets over the years and still made the trips up for the games even though the team went through some bad seasons for quite a few years, supporting as always and enjoying meeting fans who attended from all over the world. Often asked why, my answer is it's my way of showing how I feel a "DIE-HARD fan remains loyal to their team through the good times and the bad. During those lean years there were still media coverage and request for guest appearances for me which I took full advantage of especially with our records, but with each opportunity given my "Mission" was to share the fire and passion I had for my team with the world always looking at myself as that ambassador who represents win, lose or draw. I call my terminal condition "Raidertudosis", which there isn't a cure only treatment which I call "Therapy" which comes from being at a game or watching it on television. I have been in the process of treating my condition since my first Raiders game in 1983 in Los Angeles at the coliseum. What has kept me going on with my "Mission" to change the general perception of us Raiders fans is the affect I've seen on people who after breaking bread and really getting to know more about us as a fan base encourages me to strive on in an attempt to leave a positive impression with whoever comes in contact with me. In my opinion this is a way of life for us, not just something we do during football season because we carry our torches high every minute of the day, every day of the year. Understanding that this way of life isn't for everyone and those of us who cherish each other and the moments we endure together good or bad is what galvanizes us worldwide as a family.

Chapter 6

Time marches on and we continue along this journey of ours with plenty of great memories beginning to stack up and as I grow closer in my relationship with my girlfriend, I decided to take the next step as my heart was telling me that she's a keeper. My job situation was steady and financially I'm continuing to repair credit after my divorce, figured I would show her how much I appreciated her love and support through everything and went to purchase a nice ring for her. Upon entering the jewelry store and told the jeweler to let her try it on for size, I

Bertha and I on wedding day

couldn't help but notice the expression on the jeweler's face as my girlfriend had run out of the store. After walking outside to ask why she'd left the store so quickly, she told me that she wasn't ready for what she thought was an engagement ring. I explained to her that this was just a diamond ring to show her my appreciation for her support, so as we return into the store the jeweler got quite a laugh out of how quickly my girlfriend had left the store walking completely outside. We laughed about the whole scenario over dinner, as I assured her that the ring was just something I felt she deserved. But in reality, I had been shopping around for the ring that I would eventually present to her when the time was perfect, so having her accept this first ring to me was just the prelude to what was to come. The hospital that she worked at sponsored a white-water rafting trip to the Kern River and I went with her and a few friends. Again, feeling like I did on the horse in Hawaii because never had any experience in rafting, started this adventure with adrenaline on full tilt. Arriving at the campsite we

Whitewater Rafting

were assigned tents for us to sleep in over the weekend, so that night we got acquainted while sitting around a huge campfire and enjoying some tasty libations before our early morning rise. The next morning, we grab some breakfast before setting out toward the launch spot on the river, the anticipation building as we finally make it to the launching spot, put on the rest of our gear and get teamed up in the rafts. There were seven people including a guide in each of the rafts as we start floating down the river in relatively calm waters. Our guide told us some of the history about the area and prepared us as each section of the river seemed to get a bit rougher. Where we had launched he called stage 1 of the ride, so by the time we passed through stage 2 and entered stage 3 we all felt the changes in the current on the river. We hit a few drops that he had talked about earlier and navigated around several rock formations in the water, but as we approached stage 4 there was this drop of about twenty feet ahead of us. The guide advised us to brace ourselves for the drop and assured us that it would be one to remember, so as our raft hits the edge of the drop, I'm sitting up front on the right side with Bertha behind me, we take the plunge headfirst down the fall. Somehow, I become dislodged from the raft and fell headfirst into the freezing water, knowing I would get left behind if I didn't grab the safety rope that went around the body of the raft. I hung on for dear life until they could pull me back inside the raft where everyone including the guide almost split their sides laughing at my form as I went airborne and hit the water. They described it like a big cat sprawled out in the air. All I cared about was surviving the fall and not hitting the rocks that were below, another group of rafters grabbed the oar I lost during my tumble into to river and returned it when we took a short break before completing the ride. At the end of our rafting experience while looking back over the events of the one of the riders from another raft hooked the back of my life vest pulling me backwards into the frigid water, where upon coming up to the surface had to be restrained from going after him. He didn't understand why I got so angry but I let him know I didn't play around like that. He later apologized for what he had done and offered me a beer. Back at camp we got cleaned up and met for dinner and swapped stories of the day before preparing to leave for our return trip home. Also I felt that the time was right to combine our living arrangements as we often talked about finding a suitable place for us to live in town and as we watched one complex under construction on Milliken Avenue in Rancho Cucamonga I would say to her that we're going to have a place in this complex. As if I was speaking it into existence, when applications were being accepted for leasing the apartments ours was one of the first to be approved and we had the choice of units to live, so with ultimate security in mind we chose a unit with a two car garage with entry into our apartment and on the ground level so carrying things upstairs wouldn't be an issue. Move in day was exciting for us beginning a new chapter in our relationship together and the plans for the future, renting a large moving truck to load everything into our new apartment from my old apartment and the stuff she had in storage and at her mom's house. Again, as I've stated before, life was good for me as I could see myself slowly turning a corner and moving in a positive direction, with good fortune seemingly upon every turn. We continued our football road trips to Oakland enjoying meeting people from all over the world and just experiencing being Raiders fans together which had always been a dream of mine since making it to California. Through my friend Gorilla Rilla, I got to participate in an event for some at risk kids in Oakland, hanging out with them and sharing some inspiration to both them and the organization sponsoring the event. They told stories of growing up watching the Raiders games with their parents and or grandparents but never being able to actually attend a game so my friend Gorilla Rilla began taking a group of kids to the games every year. Different tailgate groups would provide food and beverages for the kids paid for by Gorilla Rilla like the Bad Boys of BBQ, The Black Hole's tailgate, D Lot crew and others. There was also lots of time spent at youth football activities, karate practices and water polo games supporting Bertha's three sons. I would remind her kids to never take the opportunity of attending these Raiders games for granted because most of their peers had never even been to a professional game and to cherish the moments as a chance to see the games from a totally different perspective than watching on television. During those youth football practices I had the pleasure of running into Steve and Marla Smith, who I knew from when my son Orlando and their oldest son Tyler played on the same teams. We had some great evenings always finding a tree to relax under while their youngest son Wyatt and Bertha's youngest son Cedric practiced. We named ourselves the 'Tree People' because we would have our own parties beneath the trees and some of the other parents looked on wondering why we enjoyed those hours under the tree. We took numerous weekend getaways to places like Hearst Castle, Pismo Beach, Solvang and Catalina Islands. On our trip to Pismo Beach we rented quad runners for riding the dunes along coast and right away got a bit of a scare when Cedric's quad slid down an embankment into a deep hole. After doubling back to look for them and successfully pulling him and the bike out of the sand went back to return the rentals and grab dinner before enjoying the gorgeous sunset. Another adventure involved a three-day cruise to Mexico with some of Bertha's co-workers where I got to meet and party with on the ship. We kicked it off with a toast in our cabin with her boss Sally and her husband Jose to break the ice before dancing the night away in the night club onboard. We took our excursions through the cities where we docked and enjoyed taking in the sights, sounds and great food before boarding to continue the cruise. Meanwhile back on the home front things quickly progressed along and Bertha and I were married in 2003, a small wedding joined by close friends and family at the Etiwanda Gardens chapel followed by a fantastic reception all with our own finances which we were proud of because together we put everything in place. I remember how amazed my mom was seeing me busting moves on the dance floor and asking my brother what had gotten into me as I did the 'Nasty Dog' dance with Bertha. He tried to explain to her that I'd been doing this since we were kids and she just hadn't ever had the opportunity to witness it for herself, so I had to get her up on the floor with me because I'd watched her and her friends dancing when I was a kid just to see her cut the rug. She warned me not try that crazy dance she had seen me doing earlier, but I was thrilled to get her on the dance floor with me. Bertha's mom had spoken earlier at the reception of how this 'Cactus' which was me, had taken her 'Rose' which was Bertha and my mom asked me what that was all about, so I just said it was a long story. That old adage about time flying when you're having fun is so true as the time came to end our reception just as we started to get loose, so we said our goodbyes and finished our celebration at our apartment until everyone waved the towel in the early morning. Later that morning after breakfast we had to take back the props that we'd rented for our reception before taking a trip to Las Vegas to finish celebrating our marriage. Accompanying us were my mom and my brother Lee, along with my wife's dad and her brother as we put a couple of rental cars through the paces up Interstate 15 until arriving at our hotel in Las Vegas two hours later. Spending the next two nights enjoying the sites and eateries around the city seemed to go by much too fast, as it was time to pack up, check out and get my mom and brother back to catch their flight back home in Connecticut. Bertha's dad and brother flew back home to Austin, Texas where they lived shortly after and got on with our daily lives together conquering work, kids and their sports activities, traveling to the football games in Oakland and myself staying busy cleaning up my credit in preparation of purchasing another house in the future. We met the Navarro family consisting of Pablo, Theresa, Ivan and Blaise while attending the football games in San Diego and became close friends over the years, sometimes meeting up at Theresa's mom 'Raider Toots' house and caravanning to the stadium and throwing our own tailgate parties. Outside of football we gathered at their house to celebrate birthdays and family events. Their son Ivan was an officer with the California Highway Patrol until his passing, through which I had the pleasure of meeting some great guys working on the force in San Diego. We have joined the Navarros at several Jazz festivals and concerts, which most of the times turned into long nights of good times and fantastic memories. We planned a trip to wine country in Temecula, California for a day of Hot Air ballooning, wine tasting and dinner where we met a couple who we partied with until we were all feeling pretty good. Afterwards we returned home with some fantastic photos and memories. Over the next few years, I received a letter in the mail from a lending company stating that I had been pre-approved for a home loan, with the amount of my approval and as I read in disbelief, looked upwards and thanked God for this blessing. It was like a timer went off in my head ticking away before we could finally buy a house together, so we began looking in our immediate area for suitable housing but nothing really fit into the budget that I'd been given so we widened our search radius only to find out that most of the suitable houses were very old, or needed a lot of repairs. Now around this same period of time a few of my co-workers had been searching for houses to buy and through conversation I came across a couple of realtors out in the Moreno Valley area, so after making contact with them started to take our house search further east hoping to find something we could both afford and agree on purchasing. After deciding to go with our preferred realtor, I began to receive about twenty houses listed for sale every day as my homework so to speak as I looked through every listing selecting the ones we wanted to take a closer look at. These walk-throughs took place on the weekends, which also gave us the opportunity to get a clearer picture of each neighborhood, but the hardest part of the house search was getting my wife out of her comfort zone there in the Ontario- Rancho Cucamonga area where she'd lived for a big portion of her life. At this point, I was more interested in finding a home that I could hopefully retire in, in a quiet neighborhood so I think my excitement level was way above hers at the time but still convinced that I could sway her thinking if we found the perfect house kept making weekend appointments to look at what seemed like hundreds of homes. As our house searching continued, we eliminated some neighborhoods early on and our realtor always reminded us that there were literally hundreds of listed properties to check out and to not get despaired over a few disappointing houses and neighborhoods. Next, we had to deal with the bidding wars as we were locked in on a particular single level house with several other potential buyers and after losing bids on two different houses and the disappointment associated with that fiasco, we pondered whether we could ever actually buy a house. Being assured by Garrett our realtor to continue to drive out and walk through the list of homes he kept emailing to me, we decided to put his confidence to the test and continued making the drive out to Moreno Valley checking this endless listing of houses which was in 2008 just after the housing market took a big economical hit. After an extensive search over several months, we found

86

Stepsons Graduation Photo

a house that suited everything on our wish list and after making an offer on the house proceeded to get the runaround by the bank that owned the property after it appraised for less than what they thought it should have which meant that we would save about eleven thousand dollars under what we had offered on the house. Our paperwork was pushed aside by the manager of the bank angered by the appraisal which was conducted by their own appraiser. Meanwhile we're paying rent at a weekly rate at our apartment because we had cancelled our lease agreement thinking we'd be moving into our new house. Not a good situation at all, so I called my lending company and told them that if we didn't get a call to come in to sign our docs to withdraw our offer on this house. Meantime the management at our apartment is trying to persuade us to renew the lease and just continue living there which I wanted no part of because I could taste finally getting back into my own home after dealing with apartment life for around eight years following my divorce. There were a lot of rules there that we never liked, two in particular they didn't let you fly any sports flags and they didn't want any charcoal burning grills on your property. So having just purchased one for the apartment told them I would move out if that was the deal breaker, so they allowed us to keep it there. Our apartment was the first one as you drove into the complex and with our patio facing the entrance people would get a good view of the smoke from the grill whenever I cooked, plus they could see it from the office. Then we had a family move in above us who let their kids stump around making so much noise I finally walked up to their apartment to ask them to respect the people living below them, but went to management when that didn't work. After that we received the side eye whenever we saw each other so we were determined to leave after being there for five years. We received a call from the lender to come in to sign our docs a couple of days later and couldn't believe the story of how she had spoken with the bank manager's father telling him about our situation and how he had instructed

Cedric
Eastern Illinois University

his son to put aside his anger and make the sale on this property happen. So after signing what seemed like a small encyclopedia of papers, we got the keys to what later became my retirement home with a beautiful view of the entire valley from the hillside. Having already reserved a large moving truck we couldn't wait to move into a beautiful home that I feel God meant for us to eventually get. I'm sure you can relate to how much fun moving can be, so here we go trying to get all of our possessions moved in over a weekend so I could return the moving truck, get back my deposit and rest up for workday on Monday. Through our ordeal with the bank, somehow the electricity wasn't turned on so we spent the first couple of nights burning candles to see. I reminded the kids that they could've lived in those days when kids had to do their homework and chores by candle light and this situation would be fixed on that Monday. Physically taxed after completing the move and getting things put away and arranged, I immediately began putting my stamp on the house adding some paint and stonework, planting some tropical plants and trees to add to the curb appeal and adding some wrought ironwork to the exterior of the house. I hated the carpet on the floors even though it was relatively new because of my allergies, so I would change it later. Next came adjusting to the drive for my wife who works in the city of Covina at a hospital which added another hour to what she normally drove before, but with my work I usually had to drive eighty to one hundred miles one way for some of my job projects so it wasn't much adjusting for me to do. Most of the time in my line of work we were sent to jobs in the opposite direction from where you lived so many times you would pass your co-workers on the freeway going to a jobsite near each other's city, which we all thought was ridiculous but had very little say in any of management's decision on where you worked. Then came getting the kids enrolled in the schools out here where we lived which came with its own drama because they didn't like the idea of leaving their friends and places they had grown up around in Rancho Cucamonga. It took quite a bit of persuading with the youngest son who played football at Rancho High School and after playing on the team at his new school in Moreno Valley decided to transfer back to finish high school in Rancho Cucamonga. There was plenty of running back and forth but we made it work and he graduated and ended up attending college in Colton, California before transferring to Eastern Illinois University where he played football on scholarship for three years. We spent those three years traveling back and forth for his games and eventually his graduation, which seem to go by incredibly fast but we could finally recover from the expense of traveling between my wife and I and him during school breaks and holidays wanting to come home until he met a good friend Vincent on his football team from Chicago who he started going home with during some school breaks and after meeting his parents felt like we had family members to hang out with whenever we made the trips to Charleston, Illinois where the school is. There were some very memorable moments along the journey, one being followed by a camera crew for HBO as we went through our preparations for game day in Oakland where we were interviewed and filmed as we drove to the stadium, capturing a lot of the rituals of tailgating before the game began. We were joined by our friends the Smiths that we met at youth football practice who are Raiders fans, so along with the media film crew had a fantastic weekend and made memories we'll share forever. After a long struggle we finally had our fan calendar printed and launched, where twelve of us had the honor of representing each month of the year. They were only published for one year even at the request of numerous fans who loved them for their children, to give as gifts and they didn't mind their husbands and boyfriends having them, which I thought was a win-win for everyone. Big thanks to my friend Ken Webb who stayed on the mission of getting these calendars published and the late Frank Denevi for the awesome photography. Hopefully someday we can do another fan calendar as an inspiration to the next generation of fans. Another event took place in San Diego with the cast from the NFL Network before a Monday Night Football game against the Chargers, where my character "Violator" and two of my closest character friends 'Toozak' and Gorilla Rilla performed in a skit pertaining to how we invaded the stadium making it appear like a home game for the Raiders. The skit ended with my character "Violator" being tucked away in bed fully dressed in boots, leather pants and spiked shoulder pads and read a bedtime story by Rich, the host of the show which was hilarious just trying to get that portion filmed without everyone busting up with laughter. Years earlier I was asked to participate in an award ceremony by Porsche where my character "Violator" had to hide inside the trunk of a small Porsche and pop out as a former quarterback of the Raiders was presented his car. I remember the degree of difficulty it was trying to get me to fit so that the hood could be closed which was impossible to do, but through the magic of television the scene came together very well. Just the look on this quarterback's face when he saw me climbing out of the trunk of this car was priceless. It was great, both being asked to participate in the ceremony and meeting the quarterback outside of a game day atmosphere. Afterwards we took some photos, exchanged pleasantries where he praised the fans for the energy that we brought to the arena. The adventures with Bertha and I weren't restricted to just football road trips, as on a trip to Austin, Texas for a family reunion got pulled over at border and had our truck searched by a juvenile scent dog who almost destroyed the interior because the smell of the chicken we recently ate drove him crazy. Upon asking one of the police to get the dog out of my truck, he responds with do we have a problem as he steps toward me with his rifle. Of course, my wife advised me to just shut up and let them finish so we could continue on our journey. We joked about it as we got back on the road saying we must have looked like Bonnie and Clyde to the border patrol. On a trip we took to the Gulf Shores for a relative's wedding, we ran into our old friend drama once again while setting up chairs and decorating this area on the beach where the ceremony would take place. We didn't get a warm welcome from the people on the beach, some even bumping us as we walked across the bridge to the sand unloading our chairs to my wife's dismay. Afterwards my cousin Sharon tried to explain to her how some of the people in that area acted and to just ignore it as much as possible. The humidity the day of the wedding even at the beach was brutal, but everything went smooth and we partied like rock stars at the reception. The next morning, we jumped on the road heading for Cleveland, Mississippi to rest for the night before continuing our journey to Memphis, Tennessee for our flight back home.

The Walk: Footsteps of My Journey

We spent some time on Beal Street sampling some delicious Bar B Que before getting drenched by a sudden thunderstorm. Upon making it back to California, we reflected on the events that occurred and the people we met on that trip and my wife got a clearer picture of what I had been telling her about my experience growing up in the south as a kid. Some of the things that were taking place in my life just reinforced my belief that God had plans for me and was just revealing it to me a little at a time as I walked along my journey which has been an awesome lesson in patience, determination and humility. I also enjoyed our trip to Tampa, Florida for a super tailgate competition where I joined my friend Kirk of the Bad Boys of BBQ, Raider Ron and entire crew for an exciting weekend of excellent dishes, great beverages and fantastic comradery between fans from almost every team in the NFL. My character friends and I were also selected to play a principal role in a nationally televised Bud Light commercial representing our fan base which was shot at a location in Carson, California. My colleagues from Oakland were flown in and I drove from home in Moreno Valley to our hotel they put us up in and enjoyed each other's company because it was rare for us to see one another during the off-season unless doing events like this. The following morning, we got up early to get in our costumes and were taken by shuttle to the shoot location where after signing all the paperwork we met with the director and a group of extras who were in this commercial. They were amazed to see the actual characters they had seen on television and showered us with positive accolades. We looked at it as another prime opportunity to represent the fans of the Nation and took a lot of pride in being professional. Upon completion of the shoot the director and his crew thanked us again for our professional conduct, stating that we behaved better than some of the actors and we all reminded him that what we do isn't acting it's what we do at every game. Lessons I feel should be shared with the people around me along this journey, thus it's become another chapter in the "Mission". And as we continued to support our football team through some subpar seasons, you could feel the momentum of our Fandom growing stronger especially with the media coverage that we got. Though sometimes not always in a positive manner, we remained steadfast in our beliefs of who we are as a fan base and continue striving to be the best we can be. Another one of those most memorable moments was when my wife and I were asked to be a part of HBO's film Sport in America, where we got to tell the story about our first date attending a football game in San Diego and the ensuing excitement of our journey together. When the film was premiered in Century City, California we got to attend it and got to meet all the other people included in the documentary and the ones that put it all together, feeling blessed and honored to be given another opportunity to share the love and to have them tell our love story as a part of this film. At the conclusion of the movie premier we attended an absolutely fantastic after party, before returning home and asking ourselves did that just happen. Another memorable experience came when ESPN the Magazine featured Football's Most Notorious Fans in the BAY AREA ISSUE where they portrayed both our game day personas and our everyday selves. It was such an honor to us because even though our football team had some less than stellar seasons, they saw a beauty in how we always brought our A game to the stadium every game. We've lost a few of our brothers and sisters under the shield over my twenty-nine years but now there is a new generation of characters who I hope will continue to be ambassadors of the team and plant positive seeds along their journeys and live to witness the harvest. I met some incredible people who worked behind the scenes putting this issue together and believe that they enjoyed the process as much as we did, and appreciate yet again another opportunity to share a few layers of our life with the world. Like I've said previously, the beauty of it all is in striving to leave some positive footprints as we walk along this journey and one by one we can bring about change throughout the world. On another occasion a few of my character friends and I were contacted to perform in a commercial for Tide detergent which was an opportunity for national exposure while we represented our notorious fan base. Those who lived in Northern California were flown to Los Angeles, but I live in Southern California where the commercial was to be shot so I drove to the set in my Raider truck. After a successful commercial shoot, the representatives from Tide and the director commended us on our professional behavior and wished us the best. I'm not sure rather politics were involved but at the last minute our commercial got pulled and a watered-down version was aired on television. Though we were all disappointed we understood that there are things beyond our control and felt like they had missed out. My work career took another turn as physically I noticed the wear, tear and grind of my profession had collected a pound of flesh as we say in the industry, but in my case it had taken an extra half pound which ended up causing me to retire after about thirty-six years as a union carpenter suffering from issues with a few disc in my lower back plus arthritis. Walking into the retirement arena was a different type of adjustment as you actually get a chance to step off the wheel running like the hamster trying to get to the cheese and basically set any schedule of my choosing, an idea I thought was just that, an idea. But what it afforded me was more time to share with some of my favorite charities helping those less fortunate to enjoy their journeys as much as possible and running my clothing line at MODO SPORTS. Speaking of working with charitable groups, one of my proudest endeavors has been helping to bring kids battling cancer, autism and other ailments along with their family members to a Raiders game in Oakland over the past few years with some close friends Smiley and Janice who have their own non-profit foundation. They work with these kids and their families on a daily basis showing them that they're not facing their battles along, and just being involved as much as I can with them is a very heartwarming experience and all it really takes is everyone pitching in and working together to share some generosity and compassion for these little warriors who exhibit such strength and courage that it inspires us to continue helping wherever it's needed. I remember Smiley telling me some of the stories and invited me one of the Christmas parties they sponsored for a group of kids and was touched by support shown to these little warriors by friends, families and organizations around the city. These battles faced by our little warriors haven't come without some losses, as we've lost a few of the kids along the way and our bond with their families helps them through those toughest times. Personally, getting involved with these little warriors has shown me how giving back in the communities is a feeling you can't put a price tag on, just the feeling you're overcome with let's your heart know that helping out when and wherever you can is its own reward. And as we watch them grow up trying to enjoy life's simplest pleasures, we're constantly reminded that there's a mission in life for each and every one of us to undertake and how truly blessed we are. Also, these young warriors are given an annual Christmas party where the families are able to celebrate the season together becoming better acquainted, enjoying delicious food, activities and entertainment and getting to open gifts, which is the highlight of the event for them. We capture these moments with pictures and videos for their families to cherish and remember the love and compassion shown to them by the foundation Raider Nation 4 Life CC. I'm proud of my friends and what they've done and continue to do for these families as the youth in their group who help with these families learn a valuable lesson in humility. This foundation also helps with our veterans as they visit them in the VA Hospital in Long Beach, California bringing them food, drink, entertainment and companionship because some of them get very little visitation from their actual families. I enjoy helping out with these veterans who have sacrificed their lives for our country, and just spending the time with them really lights up their day as they share some of their stories, play games, listen to music and roll out to admire the custom show cars parked on display in the parking lot. My friend Fritz Wilson usually leads us in prayer to kick off the ceremony after the national anthem. It constantly re-minds me about appreciating even the little things, and by doing this you tend to understand the saying, "If you can't appreciate the process; you won't be able to appreciate the destination once you reach it" because it's not the destination, it's the journey itself. I was part of Janice and Smiley's wedding held at beautiful Cabrillo Beach in San Pedro, California where the night before a few of us enjoyed cigars and drinks by the water where we were introduced to the 'Rock Crawl' a dance on the jagged edge of the beach. Thus this journey of mine has taught me to try to inspire others by showing respect and humility to the people you en-counter while walking life's path, and by planting some positive seeds hopefully landing in fertile soil, getting them moisten by our good deeds, we can enjoy the harvest as it brings us bounty a plenty to share over and over with the world. I also have donated towards other charitable causes in and around my com-munities attempting to teach by doing, hopefully inspiring just one person to take a positive direction in their life. These kindred spirits are who I call "Gen-eration Next" and it's them bringing the seeds of tomorrow spreading good deeds, love and respect throughout the land because they are our future. I also had the pleasure of meeting a young man named Shaleaf Perkins who told me about watching the 'Violator' when he was just a youngster at the Los Angeles

Coliseum and how impressed he was with what and how I represented the Raiders family. He showed his passion for the Raiders through the lyrics of the music he wrote, produced and performed and through the years I've had the pleasure of being in most of the videos he produced. I told him I looked at him as a poet who has been gifted to share messages through music. One day he said that the 'Violator' needed his own theme song and went into his studio and wrote the song, later shooting a video to accompany it. I felt honored to participate in the video shot at several iconic locations in and around Los Angeles, where we were joined by several members of our Raider Nation fan base. As we moved from location to location the excitement among us was similar to when we assemble at our tailgates and the different scenes allowed him to do some excellent editing and the finished product speaks for itself. His rap group is known as 4DUB, so check out their work as they continue to inspire the Nation's fan base with their hits. He also composed a song and produced a video dedicated to the entire Raider Nation where again I had the pleasure of being a part of, shooting at several locations to produce a masterpiece that I feel will stand up to the test of time with our fan base. Much love and respect my brothers Shaleaf and Aaron, remember to plant the seeds for tomorrow's bountiful harvest. I've also had the pleasure of meeting another group of poets out of Oakland called the Hazmat Boys who I've been in a few of their videos they've produced showing their love and passion for the Raiders and the fan base around the world and hope that the two of them, Kevin and Andrew will continue to inspire through their music. My brother Lee and I have been talking about him coming out to experience a football game in Oakland on opening day for over twenty years, in 2016 that became a reality as we flew our mom out to celebrate her eightieth birthday and afterward he would make his initial road trip with Bertha and I to the game. Firstly, the birthday celebration for Mom was great, as we cooked plenty of food on the grill, invited Pablo and Theresa along with her sister Paola and husband Barry over share the moments with our family. Both of my children Demetria and Orlando Jr. came over with their significant others and I got to see my grandson Joshua for the first time. Upon looking into his eyes, I saw the lineage staring back at me, and look forward to letting him get to know me as he begins his own journey. My niece and nephew came out from

East Los Angeles with their mom and brother to celebrate with Mom, making for a memorable evening as we ate, danced the night away. The next morning, we prepared to make our road trip to Oakland for the game which Lee couldn't believe how regimented we were in our preparations. He was brimming with excitement and anticipation of things to come, but struggled with jet lag as our road trip began. We made it to Oakland Saturday afternoon and checked into our hotel before grabbing dinner followed by a party at the Hilton Sports Bar, where Lee got to meet and get acquainted with some of my closest Raiders friends. Next morning I'm up at 3 a.m. to begin my transformation for game day, rousting my brother to get up and get ready so we could be in line to get into the parking lot by 6am. He couldn't believe how fresh I was after a hard night of partying before, but I explained to him that it was the adrenaline of game day. He's becoming more anxious as we finally get to go inside the parking lot to start our tailgating. As soon as I parked the car Lee was asked by the family next to us to help them raise their canopy so they could jump on the grill, he looks at me as to say does everyone here fellowship together and I tried to explain to him that the Raider Nation is one big family worldwide. They had never met him before, but treated him like a member of their own family which blew his mind because he said the fans didn't tailgate like that back east. He spent most of the day videoing all the festivities to show his friends in Connecticut when he and mom returned.

As each season comes and goes, we continue to make our road trips to Oakland for the games and I get to encounter more episodes where seeds are planted through my access to and with the media. Through them I've been able to show my version of being an ambassador for my favorite team doing guest appearances, commercials, and podcast spots. Opportunities most of the time you never see on the horizon as your journey stretches forward, but when presented can become stepping stones toward the destination. Another such opportunity came when I was asked to film my transformation process, road trip and tailgating rituals for the "Rituals" promo aired by Amazon coming up to a football game between the Raiders and the Chiefs. After agreeing to terms, we met near Valencia, California along Interstate 5 freeway to set up the cameras inside my rental so we could begin filming my wife and I as we traveled to Oakland for the game.

The Walk: Footsteps of My Journey

Having no idea what I was going to be doing along this trip, just following the director's lead, we ended up stopping by a cow pasture near Coalinga where we found a way to get some awesome footage of the "Violator" walking over to the fence where these cows are grazing and getting a not so friendly response from them while I ranted on about my predictions on the upcoming game. The film director thought the scene was great so after getting all their gear packed back into the van they were traveling in and us getting back in our car, set off to find another location to continue filming my portion of the promo. After traveling further up the freeway, we pull off the road at the next film location which was in the middle of nowhere surrounded by fields, farms and this long deserted road where I did an Interview sitting on top of my ice chest in the middle of the street. While the film crew set up cameras and lighting for this scene, one of the nearby farmers drove out from his house on his quad runner to our location inquiring as to what we were doing there. The crew director explained to him that we were filming a segment for Thursday Night Football and afterward he wished us well and returned to his house and we completed filming yet another portion for the promo. Packing their gear back into the van and me squeezing back into my car with all my game day attire on got back on the road to Oakland continuing to film along the way and after arriving at our hotel, finally got to take off my costume, get cleaned up and enjoy the rest of the evening having dinner and relaxing before an early 3:00 a.m. rise to prepare for game day. Once making it to our tailgate location the film crew met with us and continued to film footage around the tailgate party before it was time to take the action inside the stadium, where once again they got the finishing shots for the 'Rituals' promo. It was an awesome experience working with these guys on that piece, and after viewing the finished product felt honored to have taken part in it. We didn't get to watch it until we returned home from the game, which was the old rivalry like always, but with a playoff atmosphere and pulling out a victory following several defensive penalties in overtime was fantastic too. I got interviewed in the stands by Coach Cowher as part of the pregame show, where we talked about the Death stare he and I gave each other when he coached the Steelers as he said to the viewers, when you see the 'Violator' you know you're in the Black Hole's territory. We even had a quick dance session during commercial break, which the fans got a big kick out of seeing him boogie. Such an exciting, but stressful season where again we fell short of making the playoffs but with all the opportunities afforded me to further leave some footprints along my journey could sit back relax a little and enjoy watching this season's Playoffs only to ask myself what I would possibly be encountering had my team been able to secure a spot in the playoffs for 2018. But getting back into reality, I've always loved the level of competition that the playoffs bring because that's when the games get real. Watching each game as one team moves on and another goes on vacation for the winter. That's what I think makes professional football America's passion and pastime.

Chapter 7

As the playoff brackets dwindle down to four teams, playing in the championship games leading up to the Super Bowl in February I can't help but reflect on the events that took place, the people who I had the pleasure of becoming acquainted with and the memories made and feel truly blessed at this point of the journey, yet the anticipation and consequent sadness of the 2019 season being the "End of an Era" for football in Oakland, California where I had my first glimpse of the shield on the helmets that created the spark that lit the fire that still burns inside for my beloved Raiders! Now the two teams have advanced to the big game and with all the hype and speculations about the possible winners my wife and I got to experience the game in an unforgettable fashion as we're invited by Steve Gomez to share the Super Bowl game in Las Vegas as the guest of Constellation Brand's corporate party on the rooftop of Drai's nightclub on the strip. Always a firstc lass event with fantastic live entertainment, excellent cuisine, cigar rollers, awesome cocktails and just a great family like atmosphere. They really made us feel like part of their family and I just want to say thank you. Corona had been one of the Black Hole's tailgate sponsors for several years and it was an honor to represent the Black Hole along with my amigos Gorilla Rilla and Senor Raider. I met Sean when he was around nineteen years old during a game at the Los Angeles Coliseum, where he told me that he was going to dress up like I did. I said to him you better bring it and over twenty years we have enjoyed some lifetime memories as he became Senor Raider. Even during the off-season my calendar was largely booked up with appearances, charitable events, conventions, Television and Radio interviews time seems to move along so fast that you treasure the moments when you get to sit, relax and just reflect on the journey as chapters of my life are being composed right before me.

My off-season schedule kicks off with an appearance at the Raider Fest in Pomona, California on February 24, 2019 at the Fairgrounds where there was a gathering of Professional athletes and celebrities selling and signing sports memorabilia, taking photos and just a great experience for any sports fan. Also got to participate in a documentary being done on former Raiders receiver Willie Gault, which was an honor for the video crew to invite a group of us Raiders fans to give him a tribute on camera. The following weeks led up to another event on April 6th in Phoenix, Arizona which was the 2019 Raiders Fan Convention hosted and promoted by my good friend Mike Sommers who I had the pleasure of working with on his very first RFC in Oakland quite a few years earlier where the attendance was less than ideal and I remember saying to him just keep doing it if you truly believe and they will come. The best part about having these fan conventions is just meeting the people and the families who come out and support Mike on some fantastic events as the years went on, a kid friendly atmosphere to inspire that next generation of Raiders fans. I've asked many of the old players if they had seen any other fan base doing anything like it and to a man the answer was no. Mike presented Gorilla Rilla and me a lifetime achievement award at a Raiders Fan Convention in San Diego for our dedication to the Raider Nation. Later that month the NFL Draft rolls around in Nashville, Tennessee which is an event I've yet had the opportunity to attend, so if not attending a draft day party, have always watched from home. In May of 2019, I made a guest appearance at the Rodeo parade in Santa Maria, California where the Raider Nation was represented in numbers and we were impressed by the huge crowd who came out along the parade route to cheer us on. I was very excited to attend the next NFL Draft to be held in Las Vegas, Nevada in April of 2020 that was cancelled because of the Covid19 pandemic affecting people around the world.

After too many years passed I flew back to Mississippi in June with for a family reunion where my wife and I met my mom and brother at the airport and drove from Memphis, Tennessee to the reunion in Mound Bayou, Mississippi meeting and getting acquainted with family members some who I hadn't seen in quite a few years, and some who I'd never met. But you knew you were in the midst of family and just hearing stories from the past, taking lots of photos, enjoying some great Soul food and activities was good for the spirit. Even got a surprise visit at the reunion from Carlton, an old classmate from high school who I hadn't seen in years when he was stationed in Arizona and used to stop by my old house in Los Angeles. We got to visit the Grammy Museum in Cleveland, Mississippi to admire tributes to some of the world's most famous musicians who began their careers in the Mississippi Delta. As always, the time went by so quickly that we had returned home and had to make preparations for our next trip to Seattle, Washington for another Raiders Fan Convention on July 13th. Now what sets this event apart from all the others is this was the first RFC where we all stayed together in an Air B&B, so it kind of reminded me of spring break. Very nice house where we got to eat, relax and fellowship with each other before preparing for the convention the next day. It was our first RFC in that area, and though the turnout wasn't like what we were used to, the energy was good as we got to meet another group of Raiders fans and plant some positive seeds in the Pacific Northwest. After a great RFC experience in Seattle it was time to get back home, take a quick breather before my next guest appearance in Merced, California at the first annual Raider Nation Explosion where once again the fans came out in big numbers to fellowship, enjoy good food, great live entertainment and just keep that positive vibe going throughout the off-season. During this event my good friend Mark and I were honored with an award for our many years of commitment and dedication to the Raiders and the Raider Nation family by Raider Mob Boss and the KOS family. I've never been so overwhelmed by the love shown from the family that I had a hard time holding back the tears as some of them spoke about how we had inspired them to become dedicated fans. To everyone involved and in attendance, just want to say how much I appreciated that day with all of you in Merced, that day will be embedded in my memory forever. The following week I had the pleasure of doing a guest appearance at the world famous Killarney's Pub in Huntington Beach, California where I was met by my good friend Johnny Perea during a game between the Raiders and Broncos where being my very first time going there was blown away by the hospitality and comradery from the staff and fans in attendance. Big shout out my friends Everardo and Orlando for the years of support love you guys. As always, the case recently, I got to introduce them to my Signature Collection V57 cigars making some new contacts through networking. Being a cigar aficionado, I love having my own personal cigar line to enjoy and share as you get the opportunities to meet some interesting people from all walks of life united under the love of the leaf. Along with my clothing brand named Modo Sports my cigars brings about numerous opportunities to network with people from all walks of life who share a common interest. Both are a labor of love that I'm excited to spread across the country and eventually the world.

Later that August on the 13th, I had an interview with a casting company for an ESPN/ NFL Commercial for the upcoming football season. This was done on Skype and the agency's only requirement was for me to dress in my spiked shoulder pads and "War paint", so upon the Skype screen opening for the interview and the casting director seeing the Violator staring back at him laugh aloud saying, this is going to be good and that the people that hired them were going to love it. He then proceeds to shoot questions they wanted me to answer which I did to his satisfaction and let me know he would be in touch. After receiving a call from the casting agency to let me know I'd been selected for the commercial, I was given my hotel reservation, shoot location and itinerary and instructed to be ready for pick up at 5 a.m. on the morning of August 19th. Making my way down to Long Beach where the shoot was to take place, got settled in my room before finding some place to enjoy a good meal before my 2 a.m. wake up to get in costume and be ready for the shuttle to transport me to the set. As the driver pulls up to the hotel, opens the door to the van and says you must be Wayne and laughed. He'd obviously been given an accurate description as to what I'd look like and quickly got me over to the film shoot site. After filling out all the paperwork, went right into pre-dawn filming for some early scenes the director wanted to capture. Guessing that they'd gotten the shots they wanted I was instructed to stand by until the next shots were set up. Having done a few of these shoots over my career as the Violator, was used to the hurry up and wait times that come with the territory so when not meeting other actors and crew on the set just kicked back in sort of a meditative state thinking about what scenes were coming up next. Upon getting the alert from the director to get in place on set for the next shoot, we all were given instructions on our places within the combines of the set and I was given my lines to speak. We went through a few takes until everyone was satisfied with the footage they needed to edit and get ready for the first week of the season. After thanking the directors and the crew for this awesome opportunity I was shuttled back to the hotel where after getting cleaned up, grabbed a bite to eat before heading home. I was very impressed at the finish product after the commercial began to air on television. As always, I gave thanks for another opportunity to represent the Raider Nation and continue to inspire along the way. My next adventure began on September 11th when I was contacted by CBS to shoot a promo for our game against the Kansas City Chiefs that was part of the NFL Today show. Arriving at my house from New York, the director and I went over a few details about the promo and gave me my lines to memorize while I transformed from Wayne to the Violator. Once the camera and sound crew arrived and converted my garage into a blacked-out cave, went through their sound checks, camera and lighting positions we began shooting the commercial. I didn't notice at first, but as we continued through our takes the director kept urging me to speak my lines with these subtle fluctuations in my voice to show the intensity but sometimes a playful almost sarcastic tone to the delivery of my message. He didn't relent until he'd got me to nail my delivery, which sounded crazy even as I'm trying to focus on the fluctuations he was listening for, but upon hearing him say "That's a wrap" we all had some big laughs over how the finished promo would look. The camera and sound crew packed their equipment back into their vehicles, exchanged our farewells and the director went back to edit the footage from the shoot in preparation for the upcoming week's show on CBS. I was very satisfied with the final cut of the promo as I watched it on the link the director sent to me. This was just another stepping stone along this journey of mine. On October 4, 2019 we packed up our gear in the car and headed towards Las Vegas for the Raiders Fan Convention which was held the next day. The best part of the trip was sharing an Air B&B off the strip because we arrived earlier than the rest of the guys, so as we're parked in the driveway of the house a few of the neighbors came out to see who was sitting in front of this house. I guess being an Air B&B they figured we were from out of town, but one of the neighbors in particular found quite a few reasons to walk around his house pretending to be busy doing visual inspections to his house and a feeble attempt at doing yard maintenance which provided him opportunity to try and get a good look at this vehicle with the California plates and a Raiders sticker on the rear window. I wanted to get out of the car and introduce myself just to see his reaction but decided to sit tight until the rest of the group arrived and not bring any attention to ourselves. Later that afternoon when everyone had arrived and settled in, we commenced on our ritual called Friday nights, where we relax, enjoy great food, drinks, cigars and conversation leading up to the event the following day. The convention went well, attended mostly by fans from and around the Las Vegas area so I got to meet some new family members of the Raider Nation which is always like a reunion of sorts. There were a few former Raiders players in attendance also signing memorabilia and taking photos. It was great being a part of this event just to further show that it is a kid friendly and family-oriented event where we all got to fellowship in a positive environment as we attempt to educate the youth on how we are as a fan base. Upon the conclusion of the RFC we went back to our Air B&B to get out of my costume, clean up, grab a bite to eat and finish where we left off partying until leaving on Sunday morning heading home to prepare for another event.

October 12th, we had our second annual charity softball tournament in Long Beach, California between Raiders fans vs Dodgers fans where the proceeds went towards our little warriors' program helping kids battling cancer, autism, muscular dystrophy and other diseases. A great turnout of participants who came ready to battle it out for the nice trophy provided by the RAIDER-NATION4LIFE car club, great raffle prizes, good food and beverages kept everyone having a good time and showing how people from different teams and different walks of life can do great things when they are united for a great cause. I'm looking forward to the next tournament to win the trophy back from Team Dodgers who were the victors this year, but it's all in fun for the kids. Like I said earlier, the proceeds go towards helping our little warriors who we took to Oakland, California to watch the Raiders vs Detroit Lions at the Oakland coliseum on November 3, 2019. My wife and I went up to Oakland a couple of days before the rest of the kids and their families caravanned up because I had to attend another Raiders Fan Convention on November 2nd, which may have been the last one in Oakland since the team is moving to Las Vegas next year. The crowd was super amped because of the game against the Lions the next day, so let's just say the party was on and popping. There were several media outlets gathering interviews and footage of this historical weekend. After leaving the convention we drove a short distance to meet our little warriors and their families at a pizza party we threw for them on Saturday evening just to let everyone fellowship, eat, play games before whisking them off to bed for the early morning wake up on Game day. I would love to see the footage of the kids enjoying themselves that day. Sunday morning arrives and everyone's excited to get to the stadium where there was a tailgate party for them in the parking lot hosted by the Malosos Boosters before our group was escorted down on the sidelines during pregame activities. The kids got to meet Coach Jon Gruden, some of the players, the Raiders cheerleaders and even a few of the game officials. The most exciting part of the day for the kids was when they saw themselves on the jumbo screen inside the stadium. Overall, this turned out to be an exciting weekend for everyone who made the trip to Oakland for the game. The following week was capped off with a trip to the VA Hospital where we helped to feed and visit the veterans, a twice a year event that's beautifully received by everyone involved. Big thank you to the RAIDERNATION4LIFE car club for their continuous efforts to spending time and catering food and beverages to our brave troops, letting them know that they're not forgotten and are still appreciated.

As the next road trip looms closer, I was contacted by CBS network requesting a television interview with a few other members of the Black Hole. Soon after that phone call came another request for an interview with ESPN for an E-60 piece being aired the following week before the last home game in the Oakland Coliseum before the Raiders move to Las Vegas, Nevada for the 2020 season. Both interviews went well and after completion of shooting the videos it was time to grab some quite time to relax before preparing for the football game Sunday. On December 6th I headed up to Bend, Oregon where we had been invited to ride on a float in the Christmas parade on the 7th. This trip was roughly a fourteen-hour drive for my wife and me to complete and throw in the weather factor, made our road trip quite the excursion. It was my first time driving through snow, ice and rain at one time so staying focused was even more of a premium than ever, so only stopping for gas continued rolling on until reaching our destination. We arrived in town late the night before our hotel reservation so we ended up sleeping in our car with the engine running to stay warm until morning where we found a local diner to grab breakfast and check out the town before checking into the hotel. In the parking lot of the diner were people turning doughnuts on the icy pavement, one guy ran into another car in the lot because not clearing the ice from his windshield. We just looked at each other wondering if there was something we were missing. The warmest temperature was 46 degrees, so we definitely got a taste of winter while in town. Later that evening we went to a meet and greet with the booster club who invited us to participate in the parade, which was fantastic but short lived so I could rest up from the drive and make sure all my gear was laid out for the following morning, which has been a part of my ritual since the very beginning. As my alarm chimes at 6 a.m., it was time to get up and begin my transformation into the Violator for the Christmas parade later that morning. This parade was like no other I'd been in before and it seemed as if the whole town had come out lining the streets of Bend and cheering the floats and other participants in it. I had the pleasure of meeting Kenny King, former Raider player and chopping it up before getting on our float to begin the parade. To my surprise the float we were riding on won the first place ribbon to the delight of the Bend booster club members, and at the conclusion of the parade my wife and I said our goodbyes and got back on the road now heading to Oakland for the football game the next day on Sunday Dec.8th. I had another video shoot later that morning with a CBS film crew to gather some last-minute footage for their program.

At this point, between our road trips to Oakland and all of the video shoots and media interviews the season had flown past and now we're preparing to make what was to be the final game played in Oakland, California. I wish I could describe to you all of the emotions and fanfare that was in the air on this morning of December 15th of 2019, but in a nutshell the atmosphere surpassed the excitement that we had on opening day of this final season in the coliseum. Fans of the Raiders from all around the world converged around the Coliseum to fellowship with each other for the last time on the sacred soil of Mecca. On top of all of the fans' excitement was the amazing media frenzy surrounding this historical day in the Raiders history in Oakland. This really felt like a huge family reunion seeing the fans who had never had the opportunity of making it to Oakland for a game during the teams' entire history there putting this special day on their bucket list. And friends that I hadn't seen for years who made it back to Oaktown for one last tailgate party made this day of fellowship one of the most memorable ones for me ever. The general feeling among the fans was like this may be the last time a lot of us would ever see each other, some refusing to say goodbye but instead until the next time. Even trying to make my way through the security check points took quite a while because of the fans wanting to have their chance to grab one last photo and just say thanks for the decades of memories they had of this ambassador for their beloved Raiders. What was interesting to me were all of the security and law enforcement people who took their turns thanking me for representing the team with class and dignity. Once getting through the turnstiles for the last time there were literally hundreds of fans waiting inside the stadium trying to grab photos with me for possibly the last time, so it was extremely slow just trying to make it to my seat. I remember trying to keep my emotions in check with all of the love coming from everyone that I'd run into throughout the morning. Finally making it to our seats there wasn't any time to catch my breath because I received that same love from the staff were coming over to say their goodbyes, many who I have had the pleasure of knowing for twenty-four years and would probably be out of work after this game ended on this day. The atmosphere was electric inside the stadium long before the game began. It seemed like even the routine things were more amplified and as the planes flew over the stadium at the end of the national anthem the roar from the crowd was deafening. Most of the fans stood on their feet through the entire game as the action on the field kept us on edge because of the closeness of the scores, feeling at times I was going to hyperventilate. The mood became as somber as being at a wake, because our team was letting this last home game slip away from them. As the clock finally counted down to zero this 'End of an Era' in the Oakland coliseum brought out all the emotions that we the fans had been wrestling with the entire day. Those exciting emotions quickly turned sour after the team lost to the Titans, it felt like we had our hearts ripped from our chests, thus that feeling of being at a funeral of a

Great Grandfather:
Ed Brandon

close relative. As we all said our farewells and took one last look at the place we considered to be home for over two decades since the team's return to Oakland in 1995, my thoughts fell on how life was going to be for me not being a season ticket holder after over thirty years because of being retired with a fixed income couldn't begin to afford the seats I had previously in Oakland. But even as this Era in Oakland came to an end, the transition from "Mecca 2 Babylon" as I'm calling it had already begun, and what keeps me going are the many fond memories made on that hallowed ground for twenty-four years. What's in store for my journey in 2020 only God knows and time will ultimately tell, but stay tuned for another decade of football in Las Vegas and the beginning of a new Era. Hopefully I will be able to continue leaving footsteps along my journey. Meantime I'll continue gaining exposure for my clothing line which you can find by going to my website: www.modo-sports.com and sharing my Signature Collection cigars, V57s by contacting me through my social media sites: Instagram/@mabrywayne; Twitter/@violator57; LinkedIn/Wayne Mabry; Facebook/ WayneMabry57. Also, this last season I had the pleasure of co-hosting a podcast with my good friend David Grant called NFLNATIONLIVE, where we discussed the previous weeks' and the upcoming games for all thirty-two teams. Our intentions are to give the fans of the NFL an opportunity to get involved by letting their voices be heard, so follow us @nflnationlive on Twitter. In closing I would like to thank my guardian angels for steering my journey in the right direction and enabling me to plant some seeds necessary for the Harvest. And to those kindred spirits around the world, keep the Faith, keep inspiring and continue showing the rest of the world that we are a family. As I always say to generation next, don't be afraid to have dreams, don't be afraid to dream big, have the desire, dedication and determination to follow them, stay focused in trying to achieve them, but most of all "Enjoy the Moments of the Journey." I love you!

Acknowledgements

Oakland Raiders The Black Hole NFL Films
Steve Gomez Constellation Brands ESPN
Marc Badain CBS Sports Cheryl Nichols
Amy Trask David Grant HBO
Rich Eisen FOX Sports Joy Hemp
Bertha Mabry Cytosport Amazon
Mike Sommers Curt Sandoval Rodney Diesman
Lee Mabry NFL Network Mike Pickett
4DUB Bill Cowher Hazmat Boys
Minnie Mabry Gerald Strickland I T Montgomery
J FK High School City of Mound Bayou Lee Mabry Sr
City of Los Angeles Jackson State University Carpenters Union
Andrew Lloyd Nellie B. Hopkins-Lloyd Benjamin Lloyd Sr
Steve Sabol Kenny Stabler Greg Townsend
Tom Flores Jerry Robinson Howie Long

Wayne Mabry

The Walk: Footsteps of My Journey